GREAT MOMENTS IN
BASEBALL

GREAT MOMENTS IN
BASEBALL

GEORGE L FLYNN

GALLERY BOOKS
An imprint of W.H. Smith Publishers Inc.
112 Madison Avenue
New York, New York 10016

A Bison Book

Published by Gallery Books
A Division of W H Smith Publishers Inc.
112 Madison Avenue
New York, New York 10016

Produced by
Bison Books Corp.
15 Sherwood Place
Greenwich, CT 06830

ISBN 0-8317-4025-6

Printed in Hong Kong

1 2 3 4 5 6 7 8 9 10

PAGE 1: *Joe DiMaggio slides into the bag
after getting his 56th consecutive game hit.*
PAGE 3: *The Pirates leave the field after
winning the pennant. Center – Willie
Stargell.*

CONTENTS

INTRODUCTION

The 1986 baseball season was not a month old when a young, hard-throwing strikeout artist named Roger Clemens of the Boston Red Sox gave the game its first great moment of 1986. Pitching against the Seattle Mariners, the big Texan struck out 20 batters. And almost as impressive for a strikeout pitcher, he did not walk one batter. Only a home run by the Mariners' Gorman Thomas spoiled his shutout.

Twenty strikeouts in a nine-inning game. No walks. Clemens's performance is the stuff of Cooperstown. Not Walter Johnson, Bob Gibson or Cy Young ever struck out 20 batters. Neither did Dizzy Dean, Bob Feller, Warren Spahn or Sandy Koufax.

Clemens broke the record of 19 strikeouts shared by Tom, Seaver, Nolan Ryan and Steve Carlton, all three of whom will be inducted into the Hall of Fame when eligible. Injuries over the past two seasons had held Clemens back, but in 1986 he seemed to have come into his own. He has all the tools. Tall, strong and confident, he has the mark of strikeout pitcher. His fastball travels in the mid-90s mphs, and he has that other necessary ingredient to become a great strikeout pitcher: control. It is the same kind of control that Bob Gibson and Sandy Koufax had over their fastballs.   Clemens knew he was close to the record when, as he walked out to the mound to start the ninth inning, his teammate Al Nipper said, 'Rocket, do you realize that you're one away from tying the strikeout record?'

He got it fast, striking out the Mariners' shortstop, Spike Owen, on three straight fastballs. Then all the players on both teams stood at the edge of their dugouts. The crowd also stood. Mariner batter Phil Bradley walked to the plate hoping he wouldn't become a trivia answer like Tracy Stoddard and others who are on the end of 'who was the guy that' questions.

Three more fastballs, and umpire Vic Voltaggio sent Phil Bradley back to the bench with a called strike three. A groundout ended the game, and Roger Clemens, only three years in the majors, owned the record for most strikeouts in a single game. In over 111 baseball seasons and some 147,000 major league games, only one pitcher ever struck out 20 batters in a nine-inning game: Roger Clemens.

Clemens is just the latest in a long line of players who have brought

OPPOSITE: *Roger Clemens, the solid right-handed pitcher for the Boston Red Sox.*
BELOW: *Sandy Koufax, the Hall of Fame pitcher for the Brooklyn/Los Angeles Dodgers.*

FIRST THE NINE.

ABOVE: *Cincinnati, the first professional major league baseball team – 1868.*
RIGHT: *Army officer Abner Doubleday, whom many consider to be the inventor of the game.*

memorable moments to a game whose origin is still the subject of controversy. Back in 1909 a distinguished panel of Americans met to try to determine if baseball was purely an American game or if it had evolved ·from the British games of rounders and cricket. The panel found for the 'pure American' game and agreed that Abner Doubleday was the 'founder' of baseball. Evidence before and since that panel's finding has suggested otherwise, but it really doesn't matter. If baseball isn't a 'purely' American game, it is nevertheless undeniably *the* American game.

Clemens and all the other players, today's and yesterday's, should thank the people who put together the Cincinnati Red Stockings, an amateur team that, in 1869, turned professional. The owners paid salaries to the players,

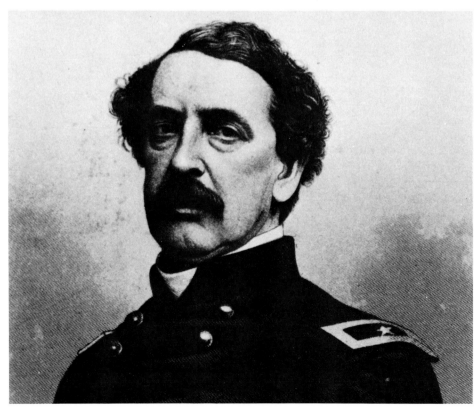

drew over 200,000 fans in the team's first year and made a profit. From that date on, baseball would become 'America's Pastime,' and fans then and now couldn't care less whether the sport came from rounders or cricket or was invented by Doubleday in Copperstown, NY.

In 1876, the same year that George Armstrong Custer discovered that Crazy Horse had his own Murderers' Row, the National Association of Professional Baseball Clubs was formed. Called the National League for short, this same league that exists today really founded modern baseball.

Other leagues were formed to try to cash in on the interest in baseball, but only the National League survived – until a man named 'Ban' Johnson formed the American League. A sports writer, Byron Bancroft Johnson created the Western League, made up of cities in the midwest. He tried to get the National League to recognize his league and have interleague games, but the older National League ignored the upstart. Nevertheless, Johnson hung tough, gave franchises to cities that already had National League teams and went head to head with the senior circuit. Finally, the owner of the National League's Pittsburgh Pirates, a man named Barney Dreyfuss, who had the great Honus Wagner on his team, came up with the idea of a World Series between the winners of the American and National Leagues. When, in 1903, an American League team accepted Dreyfuss's challenge, the last important element of what we today know as major league American baseball had fallen into place.

The nearly 83 years that separate that first World Series from Roger Clemens's 20-strikeout game have seen innumerable great moments in baseball – some awesome, some poignant, some inspiring and some just plain bizarre. Looking back, most baseball fans and historians can agree on what those great moments were, but probably not many could give you a good blanket definition of what constitutes a great moment, let alone predict when the next one will occur. Such events are too individual and too unexpected. Usually we recognize a great moment when we see it – but then again, sometimes we don't. Consider Babe Ruth's record for home runs in a single season.

When Babe Ruth hit his 60th home run of the 1927 season, there was little

ABOVE: *Ban Johnson, the president of the American League until 1927.*
RIGHT: *Barney Dreyfuss, the owner of the Pittsburgh Pirates in 1930.*

fanfare from the press corps covering the game. The House that Ruth Built, Yankee Stadium, had only a few thousand spectators that late September afternoon. The Yankees had clinched the American League pennant weeks earlier, and they were just playing out the schedule, awaiting the World Series and the Pittsburgh Pirates.

Maybe someone noted that the Babe had bettered his record of 59 home runs set in 1921, but from all reports nothing special happened. On the field, Ruth just shook hands with Lou Gehrig as he crossed home plate, tipped his cap to acknowledge the polite applause of the fans and took his place on the Yankees' bench. No fans stood and cheered and waited for the Babe to come out of the dugout for an

LEFT: *Roger Maris, the Yankee slugger who hit 61 home runs in 1961.*
BELOW: *Hall of Fame pitcher/outfielder George Herman 'The Bambino' Ruth of the Yankees.*

encore. Home runs by Babe Ruth were a standard commodity for the Yankee faithful, and while 60 was a nice round number, little attention was paid to Ruth or to his new record. Contrary to popular belief, neither the press nor the public realized at the time that they had just witnessed a great moment in baseball history.

And little did Babe Ruth or anyone back then think that three and a half decades later the whole country would be tensely watching a quiet, straight-forward, taciturn young man from South Dakota as he tried to go one better than Babe Ruth. Roger Maris would hit home run number 61 on the last day of the 1961 baseball season. The whole country would go wild, for while Maris had been advancing on Ruth's record he had been the subject of more intense media coverage than any athlete in history. Afterward, when Baseball Commissioner Ford Frick, a crony of Ruth's, announced that Maris's achievement still fell short

The splendid slugger Reggie Jackson, when he was with the New York Yankees.

of Ruth's because it hadn't been accomplished in 154 games, and that therefore an asterisk would be placed next to Maris's name in the record book, it seemed that the whole nation was split into pro- and anti-asterisk camps.

Henry Aaron certainly got plenty of attention 13 years later when he broke Ruth's lifetime home run record, and so did Whitey Ford when he broke the record that Ruth had established,

while pitching for the Boston Red Sox, for consecutive shutout innings in a World Series. No one doubted that these deserved to be called great moments, nor did anyone doubt that it was a great moment when Reggie Jackson hit his third consecutive homer in the 1977 Yankee-Dodgers Series, thus tying another Ruth record.

In fact, it is always a great moment whenever a long-standing baseball record – especially one set by a giant like Ruth – is broken. And this is not solely because of the intrinsic difficulty of the achievement. As time passes, it actually becomes *harder* to break the

great records of the past. It is worth remembering that the players who set the original records never faced the day-by-day stress their pursuers do. Most of the great records – Ruth's 60 home runs in a season and 714 in his lifetime, Cy Young's 508 victories, both Ty Cobb's season and lifetime stolen bases, as well as his total of 4191 hits, Walter Johnson's 3508 strikeouts – were marks established under no more than the normal pressure of the game. No army of writers and cameramen followed the players around as they set these marks. And the games themselves were played under less stressful

ABOVE: *Stan 'The Man' Musial in spring training with the St Louis Cardinals in 1956.*
ABOVE LEFT: *Lou Gehrig congratulates Babe Ruth on his 60th homer for the Yanks.*

LEFT: *National League President Ford Frick with Enos 'Country; Slaughter (left) and Harry Brecheen after the '46 Series.*

everyone will mention Fred Merkel's boner . . . and that happened in 1908! Every time a player puts together more than 20 games in which he has at least one hit in each game, people begin comparing his streak to Joe DiMaggio's 56 straight. And if a third baseman makes a few great defensive plays, people at once recall Brooks Robinson in the 1970 World Series. Comparing today's players with the greats of the past is one of rituals of baseball. Is the new guy going to become another Musial, is the pitcher's fastball as fast as those of Bob Feller or Sandy Koufax?

Then there are the moments that live in the lore of baseball because they were accomplished not by great players, but by unknowns, the 'good-field no-hit' player, the pinch hitter, the relief pitcher, the subs and the bench warmers. A Sandy Amoros goes into the corner of Yankee Stadium to take away a sure double off the bat of Yogi Berra and win a World Series game for the Brooklyn Dodgers against the hated Yankees. Mickey Lolich beats the wondrous Bob Gibson, and the Tigers come back from dead and win the 1968 World Series. Billy Martin has been a .250 hitter for the Yankees

conditions – in the daytime, on grass and after less time spent in travel, for the furthest west the early teams had to travel was St Louis.

The breaking of a long-held record is certainly a great moment and worthy of all the publicity and coverage given it. But there are many other great moments where no records are involved. The story of baseball is replete with achievements that stand above the rest simply because of their drama or unexpectedness, or because of the people involved.

When Enos 'Country' Slaughter raced from first to home to score on a

single and win the 1946 World Series for the Cardinals, his dash was so astonishing that none of the Cardinals knew what was going on, and certainly Johnny Pesky, the Boston Red Sox shortstop, never expected it. It was Slaughter's unexpected run that won the game and became one of the great moments in baseball legend. To this day, when a player goes from first to home on a single, broadcasters almost always mention Slaughter's score. It wasn't exactly a record, but it certainly was a landmark.

By the same token, let a player miss touching a base and get called out, and

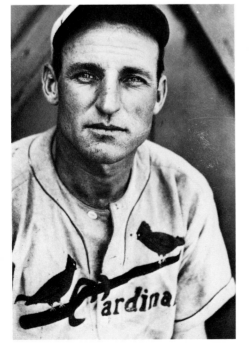

ABOVE: *The overweight pitching star, Mickey Lolich. He won three games for the Tigers in the 1968 World Series.*
LEFT: *John 'Pepper' Martin of the St Louis Cardinals' Gashouse Gang.*

all during the 1953 season, but then in the Series he hits over .500 and makes fine fielding plays that lead the Yankees to victory. Because a little-used shortstop, hitting his weight, .176, out-fields and out-hits the superb Ozzie Smith, the Kansas City Royals come from three down and beat the St Louis Cardinals in the 1985 World Series, and Buddy Biancalana has his day in the sun.

A great baseball moment can be almost anything. It may be a whole game or a series of games. It may be an individual play – a decisive strikeout, a stolen base, a leaping catch or a base

hit. Perhaps the only thing the great moments have in common is their human dimension. Whatever else they may be, all great moments are miniature dramas. Not only do such dramas have their protagonists, their 'stars,' fated to experience triumph or tragedy (or maybe comedy), but they have other cast members who, in varying degrees, are caught up in the dramatic action as well. Thus one player's great moment may prove another's dark moment. Pepper Martin's great base running literally stole the 1931 World Series for the St Louis Cardinals, but it was a harrowing experience for the opposing Philadelphia Athletics, and especially for their fine catcher, Mickey Cochrane. Until then, many people had rated Cochrane the best catcher in baseball. Fairly or unfairly, almost no one did so thereafter.

Similarly, no home run ever had the

impact of Bobby Thomson's ninth inning homer in the 1951 National League playoffs, the hit that decided that it would be the Giants, and not the Dodgers, who would face the Yankees in the Series. But if that was Thomson's finest hour, it was something else for the Dodger's Ralph Branca, who has had to bear the ignominy of having served the decisive pitch to Thomson all his life. It was even worse for the Dodger's Mickey Owen, whose passed ball in the 1941 World Series is almost better remembered than the Yankee victory it set in train.

Memorable in another way was Harvey Haddix's perfect game. Haddix, a fine southpaw, was pitching for the Pittsburgh Pirates against the Milwaukee Braves in 1959. For nine innings not one Brave reached first base – a perfect game for Haddix, flawed only by the fact that not one Pirate had yet scored. Haddix continued to pitch perfectly for the next three scoreless innings, and it was only in the unlucky 13th that his perfect game foundered in the face of a sacrifice and an intentional walk that were capped by a double. That was how Harvey Haddix made baseball history – by pitching 12 perfect innings and losing the game.

Because baseball is an infinitely varied sport, every new season contributes its share of extraordinary moments. The unconscious process by which baseball fans eventually elect to forget some of these moments and to remember others may be a bit mysterious, but in the end it always seems to produce a consensus. The moments included in this book are the result of that consensus. Whatever else they may be, the moments that follow are ones that most people *perceive* to be great. And doubtless that's as it should be, since it's difficult to come up with any better definition of what constitutes greatness.

But of course that's not to say there's no room for argument. Your own list of great moments may not be quite the same as this one. In fact it probably shouldn't be the same. Not if you care for baseball with the kind of highly personal fervor that makes this wonderful game the very special American institution it has come to be.

TOP: *Manager Leo Durocher (left) goes wild as Bobby Thomson rounds third after his pennant-winning home run for the Giants in 1951.*
LEFT: *Harvey Haddix, the star left-hander for the Pittsburgh Pirates in the late 1950s.*
OPPOSITE: *The Great Moments Room in the Baseball Hall of Fame in Cooperstown, New York.*

THE FIRST WORLD SERIES

When the American League was founded in 1901, most of the members of the 25-year-old National League had merely sneered at it. Within a year their contempt had given way to anger and alarm as the newcomers began to demonstrate that they could outdraw their seniors in such key cities as Boston, Chicago, Philadelphia and St Louis; and by the beginning of 1903 the Nationals were reduced to suing for peace. At a meeting between the two leagues' leaders in Cincinnati the Nationals gloomily agreed to recognize the Americans as a major league, to permit them to establish a team in New York and to grant them several other concessions as well.

But if a formal peace had been concluded, plenty of hostility remained. John T Brush, for example, owner of the National League's New York Giants, loathed Byron Bancroft Johnson, the former sportswriter who was the founder and commissioner of the American League. Brush secretly did everything in his power (which was considerable, given his close connections with Tammany Hall) to prevent the new American League New York team from finding a place to play ball in the city, and it was only through a combination of determination and luck that the Highlanders – later to be known as the Yankees – were able to take possession of a vacant field in upper Manhattan on the present site of Columbia Presbyterian Hospital.

In an atmosphere rife with such animosities, Barney Dreyfuss's accomplishment seems all the more remarkable. There is no plaque in Cooperstown dedicated to Dreyfuss, but there should be, for he was responsible for an idea that, perhaps more than any other, created what we today consider modern baseball. In August 1903 Dreyfuss, owner of the National

TOP RIGHT: *John T Brush was the owner of the New York Giants when the Highlanders came to town.*
RIGHT: *Cy Young, the legendary Boston pitcher, after whom the awards are named.*

League's Pittsburgh Pirates, wrote a letter to Henry Killilea, owner of the American League's Boston Pilgrims (later to be known as the Red Sox). In it Dreyfuss proposed that 'the National and American Leagues play a World Series,' adding, 'We would create great interest . . . and be financially successful.'

Killilea conferred with Jimmy Collins, the Pilgrims' third baseman manager, and Collins said that he was confident that he, Cy Young and Bill Dinneen could beat Honus Wagner, Fred Clark and the rest of the Pirates. When Killilea reported this to Ban Johnson, the commissioner replied simply, 'Then play them.'

The ground rules were quickly settled. Killilea had suggested seven games but agreed to the nine proposed by Dreyfuss. The game would be split evenly between the contenders, and neither team could use any player signed after 31 August of that year (a rule that still applies).

The Pirates went into the Series, which began on 1 October, as favorites, largely on the strength of Honus Wagner's reputation as a hitter – his season's average that year was .355. In the event, however, Wagner hit only .215 in the Series, and the Pirates' most valuable asset proved instead to be the

TOP LEFT: *Barney Dreyfuss.*
LEFT: *Bill Dinneen, the Boston pitching star.*
BELOW: *Outside the Huntington Avenue Grounds in Boston during the 1903 Series.*

arm of Deacon Phillippe, who pitched five complete games and won three of them. But three was not enough, for Boston's Bill Dinneen also won three, and his colleague, Cy Young, won another two, giving the Series to Boston in eight games.

As Dreyfuss had predicted, this first World Series was an enormous popular and financial success. It had attracted over 100,000 spectators and had earned a net of about $55,000, an amount which, when divided among the teams, came to a sum for each player that was impressive by the standards of 1903. (More, oddly, for the losing Pirates than for the winning Pilgrims, because Dreyfuss put his own share into his players' pool.)

But perhaps the best proof of how successful Dreyfuss's brainchild was came the following year, when there was *no* World Series. In 1904 the National League champions were John Brush's New York Giants, and the diehard Brush, abetted by his equally rigid manager, John McGraw, adamantly refused to play any team in the American League (which both men still insisted upon calling 'a minor league'). The result of this recalcitrance was such a storm of public and journalistic outrage that even the arrogant Brush was taken aback. In fact, nothing he might have done could have produced more popular support for the American League or have more fully guaranteed that from that time forward there would *always* be a World Series.

A pitcher who won 511 games in his career must have had many thrills, and Cy Young certainly did. Back when there was just the National League, Cy Young won 285 games for Cleveland and St Louis. (Yes, Cleveland was in the National League back then.) When the American League was formed, Young, along with many National League stars, jumped to the junior circuit because the money was so much better. While pitching for Boston and Cleveland in the American League Young won 222 games. He finished his career playing one last season with the National League, winning just four games for Boston before retiring.

Along with Joe DiMaggio's 56-consecutive-game hitting streak, Cy Young's mark of winning 511 games in his career is a baseball record that may

CY YOUNG'S BIGGEST THRILL

well never be topped. From 1890 to 1909, Cy Young *averaged* over 25 victories a season. Over 6ft 2in and weighing over 200 pounds, Cy Young was strong and durable. In those days it was not uncommon for the team's best

pitcher to pitch on consecutive days, especially in a key series, and once Young and his teammate, Bill Dinneen, won an eight-game series, each pitching with one day's rest. Young's control was legendary. He had a great fastball and an excellent curve, but it was his control that fascinated batters and fans. In 1905 he won 26 games, struck out 203 batters and walked only 28 for the season.

Pitchers like Young loved going against a team that had a pitcher supposedly as good as they. For a game on 5 May 1904 Young was matched against the Philadelphia Athletics and the brilliant left-hander, Rube Wad-

BELOW: *Cy Young, the Hall of Fame pitcher, when he was with Cleveland in the National League.*

dell. It turned out to be a game Young would remember the rest of his life.

Young was 37 years old when he and Waddell squared off. Waddell was the ace of Connie Mack's staff, and in a day when there were many off-beat characters in baseball, Waddell was so eccentric that if he hadn't been such a great athlete, Mack would probably have traded him long before. Young loved this kind of challenge – the young lion against the old war horse – and he threw a perfect game against Waddell. Years later, at a baseball get-together, Young was asked what was his greatest thrill in baseball. Without hesitation he named the game against Waddell. He remembered it this way:

A pitcher has to be good and he's got to be lucky to pitch even a no-hitter. He's got to have everything go his way to throw a perfect game.

I got fine support that day I beat Waddell in 1904. Buck Freeman, Chuck Stahl and Patsy Dougherty helped me out with good catches. I remember I struck out eight.

In the ninth, with two out, it was Waddell's turn to bat and the fans were yelling at Connie Mack to send up a pinch hitter. But Rube was a pretty good hitter, and Connie let him bat. I got two strikes on him and then he hit a short fly caught by one of my infielders. The game took an hour and 23 minutes.

In 1908, at 41 years of age, Cy Young pitched a no-hitter against the New York Yankees. In a gesture that never before or since has been duplicated, some players of the American League decided to collect donations from all the other players in the League to purchase a loving cup to give to Cy Young. It was inscribed: 'From the ball players of the American League to show their appreciation of Cy Young as a man and as a ball player. August 13, 1908.'

Cy Young later said receiving that cup from his peers meant more to him than all his records.

Christy Mathewson's 1905 World Series

There were virtually no such things as relief pitchers. Starting pitchers pitched and either won or lost. In fact, they sometimes pitched both games on a doubleheader. In one extraordinary case in 1903 'Iron Man' Joe McGinnity of the New York Giants pitched *and won* three doubleheaders in just two weeks. (At the end of the final game,

The superstars of baseball at the turn of the twentieth century were all pitchers, like Cy Young, Rube Waddell, Eddie Plank and 'Iron Man' Joe McGinnity. There were no home run hitters to speak of. When a hitter named John Franklin Baker hit a mere eight home runs in the 1914 season to lead the American League, he earned the nickname of 'Home Run' Baker. To be sure, the ball the players had to hit was softer than it would be later, when an American manufacturer named George Spalding began making baseballs. The early ball was made of Australian wool, with a synthetic rubber core and a relatively pliant horsehide covering. Most players didn't even try for a home run, but only for singles, doubles, drag bunts or stolen bases. Because the hitters didn't go for the long ball, batting averages were much higher back then. It was nothing for a team to have four or five men hitting over .333. If a player didn't bat over .300, he had to be a great fielder to keep his job. It fell to the pitchers to keep these Punch and Judy hitters off the bases.

RIGHT: *A photo of Christy Mathewson, the star pitcher for the Giants, taken in 1916.*
BELOW: *John Franklin 'Home Run' Baker slaps an infield hit for the Philadelphia Athletics.*

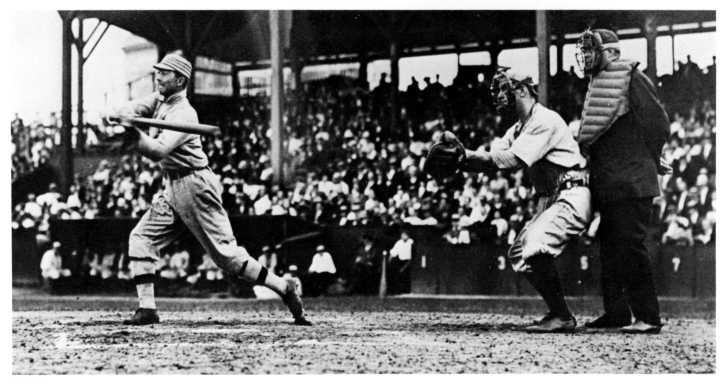

against the Athletics, he is supposed to have said to manager John McGraw, 'Mac, we still got a couple of hours before evening . . . let's play 'em a third game.') Yet even judged by the demanding standards of the time, what one pitcher accomplished in the 1905 World Series is awesome.

Christy Mathewson was probably the most popular player of his day and certainly, baseball's greatest pitcher. A tall, handsome college graduate, Mathewson was the darling of the New York Giants and the beau ideal of the New York press. He was the ace of the Giants' pitching staff, and in over 17 years with the Giants, Mathewson won 375 games, had four seasons in which he won 30 or more games and 15 seasons in which he won 20 or more games. In the 1905 World Series, Christy Mathewson would more than justify all the praise and adulation he had so far received.

After the Giants refused to play Boston in the 1904 World Series, fan anger and the pressure of the nation's sporting press forced the National League to agree to play in future Series. But first, John T Brush insisted on some new rules for the Series. This might have been a roadblock, for Brush could be an obstinate man, but fortunately most of the rules he proposed were reasonable and still govern the game today.

The Giants' opponent in the 1905 Series would be the Philadelphia Athletics. When John McGraw jumped from the American League, he had called Connie Mack and the Philadelphia team a 'bunch of white elephants.' Mack waited until the Series to make his retort. When his Athletics came on the field they had on their jerseys a white elephant with an 'A' on its body, their new team emblem. McGraw failed to see the humor.

Philadelphia had a great pitching staff: Rube Waddell, Chief Bender, Eddie Plank and Andy Coakley. Many thought it the match of Mathewson, McGinnity and Leon Ames. But Waddell, who off the field was the exact opposite of the gentlemanly Mathewson, had hurt his left shoulder while smashing the straw hats of commuters on the train coming back from Boston after Philadelphia won the American League flag. Thus the eagerly anticipated great match between Mathewson and Waddell foundered in an aisle of a Philadelphia-bound train. But the Athletics still were a powerful team, which, in addition to its pitching strength, had home-run leader Henry Davis.

It was a five-game Series. McGinnity won the first for the Giants, a shutout, and Bender won the second for the

ABOVE: *The young Cornelius 'Connie Mack' McGillicuddy – the Philadelphia manager.*
TOP: *Joe 'Iron Man' McGinnity (Left) talks with his Giant manager, John McGraw.*

Athletics, also a shutout. Under the new rules set out by John Brush, the Series would be seven games, with the first two played in Philadelphia, the next three in New York and the last two back in Philadelphia. So the Giants came back to the Polo Grounds even. Over the next six days, baseball history was made. Pitching the last three games, Mathewson threw three straight shutouts at the Athletics. In 27 innings, he allowed only 14 hits, struck out 18 batters and walked just one. Only one Philadelphia hitter, little Topsy Hartsel, hit over .250 against Mathewson. Only one baserunner got as far as third base.

After the final out, the fans poured onto the Polo Grounds and swept Mathewson to their shoulders and paraded him around the park. When he finally escaped, he went into the Giants' locker room, met with the press and showered. Later, when he and his catcher, Roger Bresnahan, walked out on the field, there were thousands of people still cheering. Mathewson reached inside his topcoat and pulled out a large sheet of butcher's paper, which he unfurled and showed to the crowd. On it, Mathewson had written 'Giants – World Champions, 1905.'

Grantland Rice called Christy Mathewson's performance that day the greatest single World Series pitching exhibition ever known. Eighty years since those six days at the Polo Grounds in New York, it may still be the greatest pitching feat in World Series history.

Walter Johnson Shuts Out the Highlanders

After the seventh telegram was de-livered to his office in a steamy locker room, 'Pongo' Joe Cantillon decided he had better do something. The team he managed, the Washington Senators, had, by mid-season in 1907, easily established the worst record in the American League. Now this guy whom Cantillon had never met was bugging him with telegrams about some phe-nomenon of a pitcher in Idaho. Cantil-lon's catcher, Cliff Blankenship, was just sitting around with a broken

finger, so he was sent out West to scout the man the telegrams said threw a ball so fast it 'looked like an aspirin.'

The result was that for a $100 signing bonus and a salary of $300 a month,

Walter Johnson came to the Washing-ton Senators and baseball. For 20 years, pitching for a team that in many of those years was the worst in baseball, Walter Johnson would win 416 games

RIGHT: *Cliff Blankenship, the catcher of the Washington Senators – a photo from 1909.*
BELOW: *Joe Cantillon in 1909, the manager of the Senators.*

and set strikeout records that would last for four decades. That fan in Idaho who had kept sending wires about Johnson wasn't too far off in his simile about aspirins. Like Cy Young, Johnson was a big man, powerfully built and the possessor of one of the greatest fastballs baseball has ever seen. Had Walter Johnson pitched for a team that had some semblance of professionalism, he might have won even more games than Cy Young.

Johnson didn't worry about having a curveball or a dropball, let alone about doctoring a ball with cuts or spit. All he did was rear back and throw. In fact, Johnson was so afraid of hurting a batter with his fastball that once he confided that he never really threw with all his power. For every batter he ever walked, he struck out four.

In his first full season in the majors, Johnson displayed a greatness in performance never before seen and never since matched. On 4 September 1908, in New York to play those ancestral Yankees, the New York Highlanders, Johnson opened the Series with a four-hit, 3-0 shutout of the New Yorkers. The next day, as the Highlanders came onto the field to warm up, they saw Johnson in the bullpen loosening up. There were no other Senator pitchers getting ready, but the New Yorkers were sure this was a ploy. Johnson couldn't be pitching again. But when the Highlanders came to bat in the last of the first inning, there was Johnson on the mound. This day Johnson only allowed three hits, all singles, and shut out the Highlanders 6-0. Sunday came, and, it being the Sabbath, Johnson, as well as all of baseball, had the day off. On Monday, when the Highlanders saw Johnson warming up, they knew for sure it was a smokescreen to hide the real Washington pitcher. Unfortunately for them Walter Johnson *was* pitching again. This time they only got two hits off Johnson as he shut them out again 4-0. That game was the first of two scheduled for the day, and all the Highlander fans prayed that Johnson would not pitch the second game. He didn't, yet the New Yorkers lost anyway. But at least, after 27 shutout innings, they finally scored a run.

That is how Walter Johnson, pitching for the worst team in the American League, shut out the New York Highlanders in three straight games, allowing only nine hits. And that is one of several good reasons why Walter Johnson was the first man selected to be in baseball's Hall of Fame.

RIGHT: *Pitching phenomenon Walter Johnson of the Senators—the first man into the Hall of Fame.*

FRED MERKLE'S BONER

In 1908 the New York Giants came back from spring training convinced they would replace the Chicago Cubs as kings of the National League. The Cubs had won the National League pennant in the previous two years and had defeated the Detroit Tigers in the 1907 Series. But the Giants still had the wonderful Christy Mathewson and 'Iron Man' Joe McGinnity, and manager John McGraw was sure they could beat the Cubs. Also coming back with the Giants was a backup first baseman, rookie Fred Merkle.

Sure enough, McGraw and his Giants entered the tail end of the season in a flat-footed tie with the Cubs. On 23 September 1908 the two teams met in New York at the Polo Grounds.

The Cubs were managed by Frank Chance, 'The Peerless Leader', and the famed double play combination of Joe Tinker to John Evers to Frank Chance was the backbone of the Cubs' defense. This Chicago team had dominated the National League for two years, and in 1906 it had won 116 games, still the major league record. Among other things, it had excellent pitching, with the staff headed by Mordecai 'Three Fingers' Brown.

In a game that had everything, the Giants and the Cubs began the last half of the ninth tied at 1-1. The Giants started a rally. First Devlin got on. Then McCormick lined to Evers, who flipped to Tinker to force Devlin. With McCormick at first, up stepped Fred Merkle, playing first base because the regular starter, Fred Sterner, was injured. Merkle lined a single to center, and McCormick went to third.

The 40,000 Giants fans are going crazy, and when Birdwell singles to center, McCormick comes in to score. The crowd explodes, and thousands run out onto the field to congratulate their heroes. Players and fans alike are milling around while the Cubs are trying to get to an umpire.

ABOVE RIGHT: *Fred Merkle of the Giants, a good player who was remembered for one bonehead play.*
RIGHT: *Johnny Evers (left) and Joe Tinker of the Chicago Cubs infield.*

Merkle, running towards second, sees Birdwell's hit land safely, and he knows it is all over because McCormick has scored. He therefore turns and runs back to the Giants' dugout, making his way through the delirious crowd as they pat him on the back.

But Johnny Evers, the Cubs' second baseman, realizes that Merkle hasn't touched second. He calls frantically for the ball and after tagging the base, calls on the umpires to rule Merkle out and to nullify McCormick's run.

RIGHT: *Fred Merkle of the Giants.*
BELOW: *Hank O'Day, the venerable umpire who called Merkle out in that memorable game.*

When Umpire Hank O'Day rules Merkle out and disallows the run, John McGraw has apoplexy. He screams at O'Day, and Joe McGinnity runs over and tells O'Day he threw the ball in the stands. He says the ball Evers has is one the Cubs' bench threw to him.

By now the crowd senses something is wrong and starts towards the umpires. Police and ushers get to them first, and they are escorted off the field, but not before O'Day calls the game a tie. The field is a mob scene, and there is no way the game can be continued.

The next day, both the claims by the Giants and the Cubs, who had demanded a forfeit because the crowd couldn't be controlled, are disallowed by league president Harry Pullman. He orders the game to be replayed at the end of the season, if its outcome would decide the league championship. As it turns out, the Cubs and Giants remain tied, and on 8 October they meet at the Polo Grounds for the playoff game. The Cubs win 4-1, as 'Three Fingers' Brown out-pitches the Giants. The Cubs then go on to beat the Detroit Tigers in the World Series.

Fred Merkle would play 16 more seasons of good baseball in the Major Leagues. He would help the Giants win three National pennants, he would play on championship teams in Brooklyn and he would end his career with the very team his boner helped, the Chicago Cubs. Yet all his seasons of fine play meant little. Neither the public or the press ever let Fred Merkle forget the day he didn't touch second base, and that single oversight blighted his life.

THE EIGHT-GAME SERIES

Hard as it is to believe, it once took eight games to decide a seven-game World Series. It happened in 1912. John McGraw's New York Giants were playing the Boston Red Sox, and the second game ended in a tie, 6-6. There were no lights back then, so they just decided to forget Game Two. Boston won three of the first four, but the Giants came back to win Games Six and Seven. The rubber game was played in Boston.

Up to the final game, many people thought the 1912 World Series was the best one played yet. Both teams had excellent pitching and good hitting, but it was the fielding that set this Series apart. Each game saw players making spectacular catches and fielding plays, robbing hitters of extra bases and saving games for their teams. But in the final game, it seemed, they sent in the clowns.

McGraw had Christy Mathewson ready to pitch. Still the ace of the Giants' staff, Mathewson had had bad luck in the series, taking losses in his other two outings. But McGraw knew Matty would win it, and at first it seemed that the fates were smiling on the Giants. They took a 1-0 lead in the third inning, and going into the last of the seventh Matty had the Red Sox eating out of his hand.

Jack Stahl, Red Sox manager and first baseman, hit a pop-up to short left-center field. Three Giants closed in on the easy out – shortstop Arthur Fletcher, leftfielder Red Murray and centerfielder Fred Snodgrass. All three surrounded the falling ball and then played 'you take it.' The ball fell to the ground, and Stahl was on second base with a double. The next hitter singled off Mathewson. Now the score was –

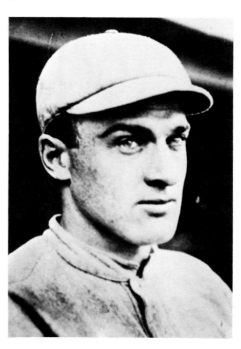

ABOVE: *Fred Snodgrass, the center fielder of the Boston Red Sox.*
LEFT: *Manager John McGraw (left) and ace pitcher Christy Mathewson.*
ROP RIGHT: *Larry Gardner of the Red Sox, who batted in the winning run.*

and McGraw was fit to be – tied.

The game went into the tenth inning. Now again fate smiled on the Giants. Murray, one of the three who had played Alphonse-and-Gaston, lashed a double to left field. Next to bat for the Giants was Fred Merkle, hoping against hope for a chance to make up for his bonehead play against the Cubs in 1908. And Merkle came through. He tripled to right center, and Murray scored. All too fleetingly, it seemed that Merkle was a hero and had won the World Series for the New York Giants. All that remained was for the great Christy Mathewson to hold the Red Sox, and Merkle and friends would be riding down Broadway in a ticker-tape parade.

Merkle, playing first base in the bottom half of the tenth, watched pinch hitter Clyde Engle hit an easy fly to dead center. He watched Fred Snodgrass settle under the ball as Red Sox fans groaned. Then, incredibly, the ball bounced out of Snodgrass's mitt, and Merkle and the rest of the Giants watched in horror as it rolled on the grass. Engle, running hard all the way, made it to second, in scoring position, and the Red Sox fans were screaming.

Harry Hooper, one of the better Red Sox hitters, took Mathewson for a deep hit to right center, but Snodgrass made

ABOVE: *Fred Merkle in a close play at home plate.*
TOP: *Tristam 'Tris' Speaker of the Boston Red Sox.*

a great running catch, and the Giants heaved a sigh of relief. Mathewson intentionally walked the next man to set up a force play, but this was risky, for the following hitter was the great Tris Speaker, who was already hitting .300 for the Series.

Mathewson's first pitch was his famous fadeaway. Speaker went fishing and popped it foul down the first base line. Merkle and catcher Chief Meyers converged on the ball and did another 'you got it' routine. The ball fell to the ground, and Tris Speaker got another chance. He drove Mathewson's next pitch down the line, fair into the rightfield corner. Engle scored the tying run, and Steve Yerkes, the man Mathewson intentionally walked to set up the force, ended up on third. With one away, McGraw ordered Mathewson to intentionally walk Duffy Lewis, another good hitter.

The next batter, Larry Gardner, hit Mathewson's first pitch to deep right field and Yerkes came in to score the winning run after the catch. Thus the Red Sox won the eighth game of a seven-game World Series 3-2.

For John McGraw, this defeat was the most bitter of his long and storied career. He would be second-guessed mercilessly by the press for walking Yerkes to pitch to Speaker. As for Merkle, his day in the sun was too short-lived to make people forget the Cubs game. And for Fred Snodgrass, there was the pain of knowing his muff probably cost the Giants the championship. All things considered, the 1912 Series was one to remember.

THE MIRACLE BOSTON BRAVES OF 1914

As baseball began the second decade of the twentieth century the most powerful teams were the Philadelphia Athletics of Connie Mack and the New York Giants of John McGraw. Between 1910 and 1915 the Athletics won four American League pennants and the Giants won three National League flags. The teams that were consistently the worst were the Washington Senators in the junior circuit and the Boston Braves in the senior circuit.

Most major cities in the country had two baseball teams – the Yankees and Giants in New York, the Athletics and Phillies in Philadelphia, the Cubs and White Sox in Chicago, the Cardinals and Browns in St Louis. In Boston, where the Red Sox played, the National League team was the Boston Braves. Few people in Boston cared about the Braves, and fewer, still, in the rest of the country.

According to baseball tradition, the teams leading their respective leagues on the Fourth of July usually represent their leagues in the World Series, since about half of the regular season has been played by the Fourth. If the tradition were correct, the 1914 World Series would be played between the Phila-

delphia Athletics and the New York Giants. And in the event, the Athletics held up their part of the tradition and won the American League title. But a funny thing happened to the Giants on their way to the World Series: They got ambushed by the Braves of Boston.

On 4 July 1914 the Boston Braves were in last place, with a forgettable record of 33 victories in 76 games. But now, suddenly, they began to win . . . and win . . . and win. By early September the Braves were tied with the mighty Giants for first place, and when the season ended the Braves were 10½ games ahead of the Giants. They had won 61 of their last 77 games in the most amazing rush from first to last that baseball has ever witnessed.

For weeks, as the Braves chased the Giants, the whole country was Braves crazy. Even in Boston the Red Sox took a back seat, and people who had no previous interest in baseball rooted for the Braves as they closed in on the Giants. When, finally, on 8 September, the standings showed the Braves atop the National League, everyone was saying how wonderful it was, but too bad that they would have to end their season by playing the Athletics.

ABOVE: *Harry 'Hank' Gowdy, the catcher for the Boston Braves in 1914.*
BELOW: *The team photo of the Miracle Boston Braves of 1914.*

The Philadelphia Athletics were considered to be not only the best team in either league, but one of the great baseball teams of all time. Connie Mack's pitching staff included Chief Bender, Eddie Plank, Jack Coombs and 'Bullet' Joe Bush. The Athletics' infield was nicknamed the 'Hundred Thousand Dollar Infield' and was made up of Stuffy McInnis, Eddie Collins, Jack Barry and Frank 'Home Run' Baker. Despite the wonderful way the Braves had come from last place to the Series, the Athletics seemed to have every right to be contemptuous of them. Connie Mack asked Chief Bender to scout them in a late-season game in New York. Instead, Bender went fishing. When Mack complained about his lapse, Bender just smiled and replied, 'We don't need to scout this bush-league outfit.'

The Braves had good pitching and a fine double play combination in Rabbit Maranville and Johnny Evers, the former Chicago Cubs star. And their manager, George Stallings, was a hard-driving, swearing tyrant who got more from his players than they knew they had. Before the first game, Stallings was talking to famed columnist Grantland Rice. He told Rice he expected his team to win in four or five

games. When Rice asked why, Stallings replied, 'We are coming, and they are going.'

The Braves won in four straight, the first time that a team had won the first four games of a Series. It was the biggest shock in baseball history. The Braves pitchers decimated the Athletics hitters, Evers and Maranville performed miracles in the field and Hank Gowdy, the Braves' catcher, hit over .500 for the Series.

When it was all over, Connie Mack broke up the Athletics. A new baseball league, called the Federal League, was about to open, and some of the Athletics wanted to jump to the new league. Plank and Bender had already signed with the Federals, and Mack, to cash in while he still controlled them, sold future-Hall-of-Famer Eddie Collins to the Chicago White Sox for $50,000 and Frank 'Home Run' Baker to the Yankees for $37,500.

The Braves didn't repeat as the National League Champions. In fact, they wouldn't play in another World Series for 34 years, and the next time they won a World Series they would be playing for Milwaukee. But no team in baseball history has ever accomplished in one season what the 'Miracle' Braves did in 1914.

ABOVE: *The 1914 Braves dugout. Left to right: Martin, Mann, Evers, Devore, G Stallings, Mitchell, Deal.*
BELOW: *Athletics pitcher Eddie Plank.*

'SAY IT AIN'T SO, JOE!'

ABOVE: *The 1919 Chicago White Sox, who were soon to be renamed the Black sox.*
LEFT: *Manager Kid Gleason of the 1919 Chicago White Sox.*

In the World Series of 1919, the Cincinnati Reds defeated the Chicago White Sox, five games to three. Baseball had expanded its showcase to nine games for the 1919 series, to get more fans to see the games and thereby to make more money. The White Sox at that time were one of the best teams in baseball and went into the Series heavily favored over the Cincinnati Reds. The Sox's biggest star was 'Shoeless' Joe Jackson, a hitter so good that only the great Ty Cobb was considered his equal. Babe Ruth, as a pitcher, said Jackson gave him more trouble than any batter in the American League. In addition, the Sox had Eddie Collins, who was sold to them by Connie Mack after the Athletics lost to the Boston Braves in the 1914 World Series. Their best pitcher was Eddie Cicotte, who had won 29 games that season. Even Edd Roush, the star of the Cincinnati team said that 'compared to the White Sox, we are just an ordinary team.'

During the Series, rumors circulated about there being a fix in, and the rumors said it was the White Sox who were throwing the Series. But at first the rumors weren't taken seriously. Everyone knew that there was a lot of gambling on baseball, that players often consorted with known gamblers and that players sometimes gambled a bit themselves. But that anyone would try to fix a major league game, let alone a Series, was too outlandish an idea to be entertained.

Yet from the play of certain of the White Sox, some reporters who had followed the team all season began to suspect something was wrong. Manager Kid Gleason *knew* something was wrong, and after the first game in Cincinnati, he verbally attacked Swede Risberg, Eddie Cicotte, Chick Gandil and Joe Jackson in a hotel lobby in front of hundreds of shocked spectators. And bookmakers across the country smelled a rat because there was so much Cincinnati money coming in when Chicago should have been the bettors' choice.

But nothing was done, and when the Series ended the Reds were World Champions. The complaints of Kid Gleason were dismissed as the grumblings of a manager who had been beaten in a Series he should have won. Newspapermen who thought there had been a fix were told by their editors to get proof before writing any more stories.

All still seemed serene as the baseball season of 1920 wound down and the White Sox were fighting the Cleveland Indians for the American League flag. But a Grand Jury was sitting in Chicago hearing testimony about an alleged conspiracy between a Chicago Cubs player, Buck Herzog, and pitcher Rube Benton to throw a Phillies-Cubs game. Two Cubs players testified that Benton told them he had made $8000 betting on the Cincinnati Reds in the 1919 Series because he knew the fix was in.

After the 1919 series, Charles

ABOVE: *Arnold 'Chick' Gandil, the White Sox first baseman and leader of the schemers.*
RIGHT: *A 1920 photo of 'Shoeless' Joe Jackson of the White Sox.*

Comiskey, the owner of the White Sox had put up a reward of $10,000 if anyone could give him proof of fixing in the 1919 series. No one had come forward until a certain gambler heard about the testimony to the Chicago Grand Jury. Hoping to get the $10,000 reward from Comiskey, gambler Billy Maharg now told a Philadelphia sports writer he knew that Eddie Cicotte had been paid off. When this story hit the Chicago papers, Comiskey and his manager, Kid Gleason, decided to confront Cicotte.

Gleason asked Cicotte to meet him at Al Austrain's office. Austrain was Comiskey's attorney, and since his office was centrally located in the Loop, players often met there. When Cicotte arrived he was asked to wait. He sat for a half hour while Comiskey, Austrain and Gleason waited in another office. Then a secretary escorted Cicotte into a conference room. Again they made him wait. Gleason knew Cicotte would be the weak link in any conspiracy, and he knew that Cicotte knew Gleason suspected him. All summer long Gleason had been on Cicotte's case, and now Cicotte was sweating.

After another half hour the secretary came and took Cicotte into another office. There sat Comiskey, Gleason and Austrain. No one stood or offered a hand to the pitcher. They motioned him to a chair and just looked at him. After a few seconds, he started to cry.

'I know what you want,' he said. 'I was crooked, Mr. Comiskey. I took money to throw games. I . . . .'

'Tell it to the Grand Jury,' snapped Comiskey, and the Great Black Sox scandal began.

When Cicotte testified to the Grand Jury, he implicated seven other teammates and named the gamblers who were involved. Comiskey suspended all eight players. Six months later, when the players went on trial, all were acquitted for lack of evidence. Someone had stolen all the Grand Jury records!

The ringleader had been Chick Gandil. He had thought up the scheme, contacted the gamblers and, when word came back that there would be $100,000 in it for the players, sold his seven teammates on the plan. All eight players had confessed to these things, but when the trial came they repudiated their confessions, and with the Grand Jury records missing, the state's case wasn't strong enough. But Judge Kenesaw Mountain Landis, the new Commissioner of Baseball wasn't buying that: He barred all eight from baseball for life, and none was ever reinstated.

One of the most poignant incidents in sport occurred as Shoeless Joe Jackson was leaving the Grand Jury hearing. Pushing his way through the mass of bodies in the courthouse, a young boy grabbed Joe's hand just as he came outside. Looking up at his hero, the boy sobbed 'Say it ain't so, Joe.' Nothing Judge Landis did could have hurt Joe Jackson more.

Babe Ruth's first Season with the Yankees

If the Black Sox scandal was the nadir of baseball as the Roaring Twenties began, two events happened in 1921 that would bring baseball back to even greater esteem and popularity. One was the appointment of Judge Kenesaw Mountain Landis as Commissioner of Baseball, with nearly dictatorial powers to run the game honestly. The other was the selling of Babe Ruth to the New York Yankees.

Historians may feel that the public's renewed interest in baseball occurred because the austere Judge from Tennessee was there to keep it clean, but in truth, the public then (as now) was not really all that interested in reform. Then (as now) the public wanted heroes. A Golden Age of Sports was dawning, and there were heroes aplenty everywhere. Tilden in tennis, Grange in football, Dempsey in boxing, Jones in golf, Man O'War in racing and, in baseball, the biggest and greatest of them all. George Herman 'Babe' Ruth had been a pitcher of consummate ability for the Boston Red Sox. But when he was sold to the New York Yankees, baseball changed forever.

Ruth had already become baseball's biggest draw while playing with the Red Sox, supplanting even Ty Cobb. It wasn't just because he was such a great pitcher: It was because he hit home runs. Fans flocked to ballparks all over the American League to see this wonder, and he didn't let them down. He hit homes runs in every park, and in 1919, he hit 29, setting a new record.

That record didn't last very long. In

LEFT: *George Herman 'Babe' Ruth as a star pitcher for the Boston Red Sox.*
BELOW: *Baseball Commissioner Kenesaw Mountain Landis throws out the first ball.*

ABOVE: *Harry Frazee, the owner of the Boston Red Sox, who traded Ruth.*
RIGHT: *Babe Ruth at bat in the first game in Yankee Stadium – 19 April 1923.*

1920, his first year with the Yankees, Ruth hit 54 home runs, twice as many as anyone else had ever hit. His slugging average for the season, an incredible .847 (or a percentage of 11.8), is a record that, needless to say, still stands. His overall batting average that year was .376, and he batted in 137 runs. Thanks to Ruth, attendance of Yankee games soared to almost 1,290,000 in 1920, double what it had been the year before and a league attendance record that would stand until 1946, when it would again be broken by the Yankees.

Impressive as these statistics are, they hardly begin to convey the impact that Ruth's 1920 debut with the Yankees had on baseball and the nation at large. That he was a genuine superstar, the greatest slugger and possibly the best all-round player the game had ever seen, was a perception that was already spreading throughout the land. But when he moved to the media capital of the nation, the public's awareness of his greatness was hugely accelerated. Popular adulation that might have taken many months, or even years, to develop came almost overnight, and with an intensity it might have otherwise never have achieved.

This is not to suggest in any way that Ruth was a product of media hype. He was a superb athlete who went from strength to strength. In 1921, for example, his second season with the Yankees, he hit 59 homers, scored 177 runs and batted in 170. He would go on to average 47 home runs a season for the next 10 years, averaging 50 for six of those years and hitting 60 in one of them (1927). But it is also true that his personality – swaggering, uncouth, yet strangely lovable and, above all, in-

credibly magnetic – was a sportswriter's dream. By the end of that spectacular first season with the Yankees, Ruth had not only come to personify baseball, he had, with the help of his awed admirers in the press, for all time transformed it into America's favorite spectator sport.

Why would the Boston Red Sox ever have sold their best player, the one who filled stadiums wherever they played? Simple. Money. Their owner, Harry Frazee, had an eye for chorus girls and had run though his considerable fortune backing Broadway shows for whose scores he seemed to have had an infallibly tin ear. His Red Sox were his prize, but he loved the girls more. So he offered his number one player to Colonel Jacob Ruppert for the then unheard of sum of $125,000. The good Colonel paid, and the rest, as they say, is history.

A few years later Frazee and a couple of his girl friends were coming out of a speakeasy late one night in the dead of a Boston winter. He hailed a cab and told the driver to take them to Fenway Park.

'The park's closed,' said the cabbie.

'I know that, just drive,' answered Frazee.

When they got to Fenway, Frazee and the girls got out. 'I used to own this park,' bragged Frazee to the girls.

'Is your name Frazee?' asked the cabbie.

On being told that it was, the cabbie got out of his hack, walked over to Frazee and belted him.

'You traded Babe Ruth, ya bum ya,' said the driver. Turning from the sprawled former Red Sox owner to the girls, he added 'I'll take you back to where I picked you up, but this bum walks.'

The player whom the record books say is the greatest hitter (as opposed to slugger) of them all was purchased from a minor league team in Augusta for $750. The Detroit Tigers paid that in 1905 for 18-year-old Tyrus Raymond Cobb. For the next 24 years, Ty Cobb would establish records. Of course, records are made to be broken. In 1985 Pete Rose of the Cincinnati Reds broke Cobb's lifetime hits record, and in the early 1960s Maury Wills of the Los Angeles Dodgers broke Cobb's season stolen base record. In the 1970s it was Lou Brock who passed the Georgia Peach's lifetime stolen base record. In each case, the player was deserving and talented, but in no way will the three of them, Rose, Wills or Brock, ever be compared to the fiery terror who dominated baseball for a quarter of a century.

His lifetime batting average was .367! Once every decade, it seems, we have a superstar who hits over .350, and he is immediately ready for the Hall of Fame. Cobb averaged .367 for 24 years. *Three times* he hit over .400, and baseball's last .400 hitter was Ted Williams, in 1941.

Ty Cobb was more than just dry statistics and records. He was the embodiment of what *competitor* means. Cobb was mentally tougher and quicker than any player in baseball, and he was probably the most hated and feared player in the game. Many of his Tigers' teammates felt so strongly about him that when he became player-manager of the Tigers there was threatened mutiny until Cobb finally eased up.

Because he could do so many things better than anyone else, Cobb was unforgiving of players with less talent. Mean, bull-headed, daring and unpredictable, Ty Cobb was a great all-round player. He could find more ways to win than anyone, and he didn't care how he did it. It took a very courageous fielder to try and tag out a sliding Cobb, and more than one had his arm or stomach slashed by Cobb's spikes. Tigers fans may have loved Ty Cobb, but elsewhere in the American League most fans detested him, even while grudgingly admiring his talent.

When Babe Ruth began hitting home runs over fences and brought the long ball to the game, Ty Cobb was openly disdainful. Ruth also often stuck out, and to a purist like Cobb, no home run could make up for a man striking out with runners in scoring position. Cobb often told reporters that hitting home runs wasn't hard. It was the single stretched into a double, the double stretched into a triple, the base running that caused outfielders to panic and misplay the ball – that was

TY COBB'S HOME RUN RECORD

baseball for Ty Cobb.

The more Babe Ruth and the other sluggers hit the ball out of the park, the more Cobb sneered. One day in May 1925, while playing in St Louis, Cobb was talking to some reporters by the batting cage during the Tigers' batting practice before the afternoon game. Some forgotten writer mentioned that Ruth had hit another home run the day before. Cobb bristled and said, 'I've said hitting home runs is easy, and I'll prove it today. Just watch.'

Word quickly spread through the press box, and more than a few bets were made between the Detroit and St Louis writers. This was, incidentally, not particularly hostile betting, for Cobb had a surprisingly good relationship with the press. He was straightforward, didn't pull punches and always had an opinion about anything and anybody in the game. That made the writers' jobs a lot easier, and since Cobb was perhaps the game's greatest

BELOW: *Tyrus Raymond 'Ty' Cobb, 'The Georgia Peach,' batting for the Detroit Tigers.*

ABOVE: *Cobb slides into third with a stolen base on a close play.*
RIGHT: *Cobb waits his turn at bat in Detroit – a photo from 1916.*

player, as well as its most controversial, he always made good copy.

On his first time at bat Cobb backed up his boast and smashed a home run over the rightfield wall. Next time up, same thing and same place. In his next three times up, Cobb had two singles and a double. When he came up in the eighth, even the St Louis fans stood and applauded, for by that time he had five hits and two homers and had driven in seven Tiger runs. To show the fans how much he appreciated their applause, Ty Cobb hit his third home run of the game. He had tied the single-game home run record, and he had also set a new record of 16 total bases.

Ty Cobb was 38 years old on that day in May. One wonders how many home runs Ty Cobb would have hit had he not disdained to do so. Maybe Babe Ruth would have been chasing Ty Cobb.

'OLD PETE' STRIKES OUT LAZZERI

The St Louis Cardinals have a long and admirable history. They have won more World Series than any team in baseball except the New York Yankees. They have more former players in the Hall of Fame than any team except the New York Yankees. Yet in head-to-head World Series competition, the Cardinals are the only team to have an edge over the Bronx Bombers, three Series to two. Of these five notable contests, the first may have been the best of all.

The Cardinals came into the National League in 1901. For the next 25 years they never finished first and usually were in the bottom half of the league. Experts said that you couldn't win in St Louis because the summers were too hot. The experts were half right about St Louis in the summer: The heat and humidity *is* overpowering. But the experts were wrong about the winning, as was about to be demonstrated in 1926, when the Cardinals made their greatest player, Rogers Hornsby, their manager.

At the same time, in Chicago, a great pitcher was nearing the end of his career. Grover Cleveland Alexander, 'Old Pete,' was, along with his rival, Christy Mathewson, one of the best pitchers in the National League. But 'Old Pete' and training rules didn't mix. Cubs manager Joe McCarthy wanted a sober, businesslike approach to the game. His rules and Old Pete's personal habits couldn't be made to conform, so in the end, Alexander was traded to St Louis. And with that the Cardinals really took off.

Baseball experts who saw Rogers Hornsby play have called him the greatest right-handed hitter of all time. His statistics back their claim. In 1924 he hit an incredible .424, still baseball's highest one-season average. He was National League batting champion for six consecutive years, and for five years, from 1921 to 1926, Hornsby's batting average was .402! In addition,

TOP LEFT: *The great hitter and manager of the St Louis Cardinals in 1926 – Rogers Hornsby.*
TOP RIGHT: *Grover Cleveland 'Old Pete' Alexander when he was pitching for the Chicago Cubs.*
RIGHT: *Taylor Douthit was first to bat against the Yankees in the 1926 Series.*

ABOVE: *Tony Lazzeri as he was struck out by Alexander with the bases loaded in the seventh.*

Hornsby was a slugger, hitting over 300 home runs, and nine times he led the league in slugging percentage. A good fielder, Hornsby is almost always the choice for the second baseman on any all-time All Star team.

The team that Hornsby put together had other fine hitters. Sunny Jim Bottomley was a star in his own right, and third baseman Les Bell was one of the best in baseball. The pitching was strong, and when Hornsby got Alexander from the Cubs, the Cardinals had a team good enough to win St Louis its first National League pennant.

But the team the Cardinals had to face in the 1926 World Series was the New York Yankees. Most of the players on that team would be part of the 1927 Yankees, now considered the greatest team ever. Babe Ruth, Lou Gehrig, Earl Combs, Tony Lazzeri, Mark Koenig and Joe Dugan were the hitting stars of this powerhouse, and the fine pitching staff was led by Herb Pennock and Waite Hoyt.

The Yankees were heavily favored, and no one was surprised when Herb Pennock outpitched Bill Sherdel 2-1, in the opening game at Yankee Stadium. But in Game Two, Old Pete evened the Series as he pitched the Cardinals to victory 6-2. The Series then shifted to St Louis, and the Cardinals won the third game as Jesse Haines shut out the Bombers 4-0.

Thus far in the Series Babe Ruth had been a bust. The Cardinals pitchers seemed to have his number, and the New York press began riding Ruth. With the shutout in the third game, the Cardinals had held Ruth to no home runs and no runs batted in. But that would change in Game Four. Ruth homered on his first time at bat, hitting the ball over the centerfield roof at Sportsman's Park. In the third inning Ruth put another one in the rightfield bleachers. Now the Yankees, led by Ruth, woke up, and when Ruth came to bat in the eighth, they had a 9-4 lead over the Cardinals. Ruth made it 10-4 as he hit still another one into the centerfield bleachers. As he trotted around the bases, the St Louis fans stood as one and applauded this marvel. Three home runs in three at bats in a World Series game. Forty years would pass before that feat would be matched.

Ruth's example held as the Yankees' Herb Pennock pitched the Yankees ahead in the fifth game, beating Sherdel for the second time 3-2. But then Alexander stopped the Yankees in the sixth game as the Cardinals evened the Series, beating the Yankees 10-2 in New York.

Now came the seventh game. Alexander had brought the Cardinals back, and, in typical Old Pete fashion, he had apparently celebrated overmuch and the next day was obliged to rest in the bullpen at Yankee Stadium. The Cardinals led 3-2 going into the seventh inning, and Jesse Haines seemed to be outpitching Waite Hoyt, when suddenly the Yankees got something going. Earl Combs walked and was sacrificed to second. That brought up Babe Ruth, who was promptly walked. Bob Meusel forced Ruth, but, pitching carefully, Haines walked Lou Gehrig. And that brought up Tony Lazzeri, considered by many the best clutch-hitter of the Yankees.

Hornsby walked to the mound from his second base position, and, after a brief conversation, signaled to the bullpen. Old Pete picked up his glove and shuffled towards the mound, the perfect image of a man with a larger-than-life hangover.

Old Pete wanted the Yankees to think that. Actually, he claims that on the previous night he had gone straight to bed because Hornsby had told him to be ready if needed. And was he ready! His first pitch was a curve and called a ball. The next pitch Lazzeri drove deep down the leftfield line, curving foul. Strike one. The next pitch was a curve, and Lazzeri swung and missed. Strike two. Lazzeri backed out of the box and looked for a signal. He got none – what do you tell a hitter with the bases loaded? Alexander leaned in, got his sign and threw a wicked curveball. Lazzeri swung, missed and the Cardinals were out of the inning.

In the ninth, the Yankees' last chance, they sent up Combs, Koenig and Ruth. Alexander got Combs and Koenig and walked Ruth. Gehrig was the next batter. One swing could now win the Series for the Yankees. But for reasons known only to himself, Babe Ruth now tried to steal second. He was easily thrown out, and suddenly the Cardinals had won their first World Championship.

Ruth had hit four home runs in the Series, a memorable three in a row in Game Four. But it was Grover Cleveland 'Old Pete' Alexander, who, at 40 years of age, was the man everyone would remember best whenever the 1926 Series was talked about.

The Athletics Win the 1929 Series

Baseball historians rate the 1927 Yankees as the greatest team ever to play the game. Babe Ruth, Lou Gehrig, Earl Combs, Bob Meusel and Tony Lazzeri were the batting stars. All five hit over .300 that year, and Ruth had 60 home runs, while Gehrig had 47. Their pitchers were Herb Pennock (19-8), Waite Hoyt (22-7), Wilcy Moore (19-7) and Urban Shocker (18-6).

In the 1927 World Series the Yankees faced the Pittsburgh Pirates. Legend has it that the Pirates came out early to watch the Yankees at batting practice. The Pirates were the home team for the opening game, and they were curious to see how the Yankees would hit in the much bigger Forbes Field. Of course all the Pirates had heard about Ruth and Gehrig and the rest of 'Murderers' Row,' but they had never played against them. As Ruth and Gehrig and the other Yankees hit pitch after pitch over the Pittsburgh fences, the Pirates knew they were in trouble. They were correct: The Yankees swept the Series.

In 1928, the Yankees got revenge on the Cardinals for the upset in 1926 and won four in a row to capture their second straight championship.

But in 1929 the great Crash of the American economy was matched in baseball when the mighty Yankees failed to win the American League title. They were beaten out by the Philadelphia Athletics, who also had a stellar line-up, with hitters led by Jimmy Foxx, Al Simmons, Mule Hass and Mickey Cochrane, and a pitching staff headed by the great Lefty Grove, George Earnshaw and Howard Ehmke. Thus it was to be the Athletics whom the Chicago Cubs would face in the 1929 Series.

The Cubs were a talented team, led by Rogers Hornsby, Charlie Grimm, Hack Wilson and Kiki Cuyler and pitchers Charlie Root and Guy Bush. The first two games of the Series were played in Chicago and the Athletics won both. The Series then shifted to Philadelphia, and the Cubs won the third game.

In Game Four, it looked as if the Cubs would tie the Series. Going into the seventh inning, the Cubs led 8-0. Old Shibe Park was very quiet when the Al Simmons came to the plate. The approximately 500 Chicago fans who had traveled to the City of Brotherly Love were the only ones making noise in the ball park. They had reason to cheer, for Charlie Root was mowing down the Athletics' hitters, while Charlie Grimm, Rogers Hornsby and Hack Wilson were pounding every Philadelphia pitcher. Very few of the Athletics' fans stood for the traditional seventh inning stretch.

Simmons hit Root's first pitch on top of the pavilion roof, and as he trotted around the bases, the faithful gave him a round of applause. At least they knew they now wouldn't be shut out. Then Jimmy Foxx singled to right, and Bing Miller singled to center. Jimmy Dykes kept it going with a single, scoring Foxx, and when shortstop Joe Boley singled to drive in Miller, old Shibe

ABOVE: *Robert Moses 'Lefty' Grove, the star pitcher of Connie Mack's Philadelphia Athletics.*
BOTTOM: *Norm McMillan of the Cubs heads for second in the fourth game of the Series.*

Park's foundation was shaking as the Philadelphia fans went crazy.

Root finally got an out when pinch-hitter George Burns popped up to short. But the next hitter, Max Bishop, singled, and Dykes scored. With only one out, the Athletics had cut the Cubs' eight-run lead in half. Cubs manager Joe McCarthy knew that Charlie Root had had it, so now he brought in veteran left-hander Arthur Nehf to pitch to Mule Hass.

With two men on, Hass stepped into the batters' box. Nehf finished his warm-up and faced Hass. His first pitch was smashed by Hass to deep

ABOVE: *Game One, ninth inning of the '29 Series. The Athletics' Mickey Cochrane and Al Simmons score.*
RIGHT: *Jimmy Foxx of the Athletics.*

center field. Squat, heavy Hack Wilson, the Cubs' centerfielder, turned and raced for the centerfield wall. Turning, he moved toward the arcing ball and then suddenly lost it in the bright sun. The ball almost hit Wilson in the head, and as it rolled away the two base runners scored, and by the time it was back in play, Hass had flown around the bases to score an inside-the-park home run. Cubs-8, Athletics-7.

The din from the screaming fans could be heard in Liberty Bell Park. Now Mickey Cochrane, one of baseball's best catchers, came up, and the understandably upset Nehf promptly walked him. Manager McCarthy at once pulled Nehf and brought in 'Sheriff' Blake to stem the tide of Connie Mack's team. Al Simmons, up for the second time in the inning, greeted the Sheriff with a single to left, and when 'Double X' Jimmy Foxx singled to right for his second hit of the inning, Cochrane scored, and it was all tied up at 8.

McCarthy is beside himself, and those proper Philadelphians are tearing the ball park down. McCarthy yanks the Sheriff and brings in Pat Malone to pitch to Bing Miller. His first pitch hits Miller in the ribs and the bases are loaded. Up to bat comes Jimmy Dykes.

Dykes had singled on his first time up to drive in a run, and now, after looking at a few Malone pitches, he lines a screaming drive down the left-field line. Riggs Stephenson, the Cubs' leftfielder, races over, and though he catches the ball, he can't hold on to it, and it drops at his feet. Simmons and Foxx score, and the Athletics go ahead 10-8. Malone gets the next two Philadelphia hitters, but it is too little, too late.

Never in the history of the World Series, before or since, has a team scored 10 runs in one inning, and certainly never when trailing 8-0.

The Athletics went on to win the fifth game of the Series and win the championship of baseball. The Athletics would repeat as World Champions in 1930, beating the St Louis Cardinals, and go into the 1931 season as the 'greatest' team in baseball. The Chicago Cubs would appear in the World Series four more times in the next 55 years but would never win a Series. Perhaps the ghost of their own 'Crash of '29' haunts them still.

PEPPER MARTIN STEALS THE 1931 SERIES

After the Philadelphia Athletics won the World Series in 1929 and 1930 some self-appointed experts began calling them the greatest team of all time. Their manager and owner, Connie Mack, told the experts to wait. Mack said, 'No team should be called great until they have won the World Series at least three times in a row.' Mack's 1931 Athletics were heavily favored to do just that as the October classic rolled around, since they were facing almost the same St Louis Cardinals team they had beaten for the championship in 1930.

Almost the same team, but not exactly. There was one special difference. A young, raw-boned Oklahoma farm boy had joined the Cardinals from the far-flung reaches of that fine Cardinals farm system that had been developed by the genius of Branch Rickey. His name was John 'Pepper' Martin; and when the 1931 World Series was over many thousands of words would be written about the exploits of this 'Wild Horse of the Osage.'

Martin's hell-for-leather play captured the imagination of America. This farm boy from the dust bowl was running and hitting like a man possessed. He hit .300 in his rookie year and helped the Cardinals beat out the New York Giants for the pennant. Of course there had been more to it than Martin. The Cardinals had Chick Hafey, who had won the National League batting title that year by beating out both the Giants' Bill Terry and his teammate Jim Bottomley by just tenths of a point. Frankie Frisch, the manager and second baseman, was considered one of the best in baseball at his position. And Wild Bill Hallorhan, Burleigh Grimes and Paul Derringer headed up the Cardinals' excellent pitching staff.

The Athletics won the first game in St Louis 6-2. But in Game Two, Martin energized the Cardinals when he singled, stole second, then third and scored on a sacrifice fly. Another Martin hit and steal, followed by a base hit, gave the Cards a 2-0 victory. When they won Game Three in Philadelphia, the Cards had a one-game lead. But in Game Four, George Earnshaw of the Athletics kept Martin off the bases and shut out the Cardinals 3-0.

Mickey Cochrane, the great Athletics catcher, had been getting hell from the press and the Philadelphia fans. After Game Four, when Martin was held quiet, Cochrane told the press that the Athletics now knew what to do to stop Martin. But in Game Five, Martin beat out a bunt and then stole second, yelling to Cochrane as he went, 'Hey Mickey, here I go!' He scored, and in the sixth he hit a home run, and in the eighth he singled.

The Athletics came back to win Game Six 8-1, so, on 10 October 1931, the seventh and final game of the Series would determine if Connie Mack's Philadelphia Athletics were indeed the greatest team of all time. The Cards jumped to a four-run lead by the end of the third inning and held off a desper-

TOP: *John 'Pepper' Martin as he looked in the 1931 World Series.*
ABOVE LEFT: *Frankie Frisch of the St Louis Cardinals steals second in the 1931 Series.*
LEFT: *Jimmy Foxx of the Athletics scores the first run of the sixth game of the Series.*

ABOVE: *Martin scores in the seventh inning of the second game of the 1931 World Series.* RIGHT: *Al Simmons of the Athletics is tagged out in an attempted steal.*

ate Philadelphia rally. In the ninth inning the Athletics scored two, and with two men on base, Max Bishop laced a line drive to left center. Can you guess who caught the ball for the final out? In this Series Martin had batted .500. He had had 12 hits, of which one was a homer and five others were doubles. He had stolen five bases, and his base running in general totally disrupted the Philadelphia Athletics. Mickey Cochrane, one of the Athletics' premier hitters, was so upset by Martin that he hit only .180 in the seven games.

During the winter banquet season, when Cochrane was the guest of honor at a dinner in New York where he received an award, the New York press serenaded Cochrane with this song:

Watch out, Mickey, here comes Pepper Martin.
If you don't watch out, he'll steal your jock for sartin. . . .

LOU GEHRIG'S FOUR CONSECUTIVE HOME RUNS

About an hour before the Yankees took the field, first baseman Wally Pip told manager Miller Huggins that he didn't feel well. So when he was writing in his starting line-up, Huggins wrote in the name, 'Gehrig, Lou,' next to 'First Baseman.' The date was 1 June 1925, and for the next 14 years, every Yankees manager would write in that same name. Of all the records in baseball history, Gehrig's string of 2130 consecutive games played is the least likely to be surpassed. They called him the 'Iron Horse,' and there probably has never been a better nickname for a player. Strong, durable, polite and hugely talented, Lou Gehrig may have been the greatest Yankee of them all.

Lou Gehrig established several batting records during his memorable career with the Yankees. Many considered him the best clutch hitter in baseball, and that was when he was on the same team as the immortal Babe Ruth. Twenty three times Lou Gehrig came to bat with the bases loaded and drove in the base runners with grand-slam homers. He set the American League runs-batted-in record with 184 in 1931. In World Series competition, where the pressure is the toughest, Lou Gehrig hit over .361 in seven World Series. His lifetime average was .340, and he was rated one of the best-fielding first basemen in baseball.

Gehrig never got the headlines or

ABOVE: *Miller Huggins, the long-time manager of the New York Yankees.*
OPPOSITE TOP: *Lou Gehrig, 'The Iron Man' and first baseman of the Yankees.*
BELOW: *A young Lou Gehrig warms up at second base in spring training.*

adulation that the more flamboyant Ruth received, but on one day in 1932 Lou Gehrig accomplished something that neither Ruth nor any other player had ever done: He hit four consecutive home runs in one game. Against the defending American League champions, the Philadelphia Athletics, Gehrig led the Yankees to a football-like score, 20-13. When Gehrig hit home run number three, he became the first man in baseball to have hit three home runs in a game four times. His fourth home run was a mammoth shot to the deepest part of Shibe Park.

The fact that Babe Ruth got most of the headlines never bothered the phlegmatic Gehrig. He knew how good he was, as did Ruth and his Yankee teammates. And on this day of 4 June 1932 Gehrig thought that for once he probably would get the headlines. But Lou Gehrig had to wait again, because on that day the headlines told of only one thing: that the police had captured the kidnap-murderer of the Lindbergh baby.

After an absence from the World Series for three years, the Yankees won the American League flag and played the Chicago Cubs in the fall classic. The 1932 Series was marked by some spirited bench jockeying between the two teams. The Cubs ridiculed Ruth, calling him Tubby and Lard and some more earthy names, and the Yankees returned the compliments with interest. Earlier in the season the Yankees had traded Mark Koenig to the Cubs. Koenig, a teammate popular with the Yankees, had helped the Cubs win the National League pennant. After the Cubs won their flag they voted on which players would receive shares of their World Series purse, and they voted Koenig a mere quarter of one share of their winnings. When the Yankees read that they were all too

THE BABE CALLS HIS SHOT

ready to call the Cubs cheapskates, misers and worse.

After two Yankee victories in the first two games, the Series came to Chicago. Over 51,000 fans crowded Wrigley Field and the temporary

bleachers that the Cubs had put up for the extra crowd. In the crowd was the new Democratic candidate for president, Governor Franklin D Roosevelt of New York. The Chicago fans, very much aware of the bad feeling between the two teams, got on the Yankees something fierce. The Yankees retaliated in the batting practice before the game by putting on a home run demonstration for the Chicago faithful. Gehrig and Ruth put balls where no Cub had ever hit them, depressing the Cubs and their fans equally.

Charlie Root, the Cubs' ace, was the starting pitcher. The Cubs needed a win to get back into the Series and counted on the veteran Root. Charlie got the first batter, Combs, to hit a grounder to shortstop Bill Jurges. The Cubs fans' cheers were short-lived as Jurges threw the ball over Charlie Grimm's head at first, and Combs took second. Then Root walked Joey Sewell, and Babe Ruth came to bat. Root, pitching carefully, threw two balls to Ruth. His third pitch eventually landed on top of the new temporary bleachers. As Ruth circled the bases he yelled a few choice terms at the Cubs dugout. Root got the rest of the Yankees in that inning, but in Gehrig's second at bat he drove Root's fastball deep into the rightfield bleachers, and the Yankees led 4-1.

In their half of the third, behind Kiki Cuyler and Charlie Grimm, the Cubs got back into the game with two runs. Trailing 4-3, they tied the game in their fourth when Jurges slashed a liner to right field. Ruth tried to make a shoestring catch, but the ball got by him, and Jurges ended up on second. As Ruth returned to his position, he was greeted with lemons and apples and other debris. Ruth tipped his cap to show his appreciation. Jurges scored on an error, and the Chicago Cubs fans stood and shouted themselve hoarse.

When Ruth came to bat in the fifth, a fan threw a lemon at him. It missed, but as it rolled towards home plate the Cubs players and fans roared with laughter. Stepping into the box, Ruth faced Root. The first pitch was a strike, and as the fans cheered, Ruth stepped back and pointed his bat towards center field. More boos and laughter cascaded down from the stands of Wrigley Field. Root threw, and again it was a strike. Ruth repeated his brag, pointing with his bat towards the centerfield bleachers. The Cubs' bench and fans were screaming at Ruth, taunting him. Charlie Root threw the next pitch, and the sound of Ruth's bat on the ball was enough to tell all 51,000 that Ruth had made good his boast. He had hit a home run exactly to the spot where he had pointed. As the ball disappeared in the centerfield bleachers, Ruth majestically trotted around the bases. As he approached third, he looked into the Cubs dugout and winked.

Poor Charlie Root. Before Manager Charlie Grimm could replace him he had to face Lou Gehrig, and Gehrig added insult to injury with his second home run of the game. The Yankees won 7-5 and then won Game Four to sweep the Cubs.

The home run that Ruth called was also his last World Series home run. The man who brought Babe Ruth to New York, Colonel Jake Ruppert, had decided to drop baseball's biggest star, and in 1934 he sold the Babe to the Boston Braves. Babe Ruth was now a washed up, overweight, slow-footed shadow of himself. He was hitting a miserable .188 when the Braves came into Pittsburgh for a series with the Pirates. The fans who attended that game came away with something to remember. Ruth, for one shining day, recalled the past and thrilled the audience with three consecutive home runs. The next day he retired.

ABOVE: *A painting by artist Robert Thom of Ruth calling his shot in Wrigley Field.*
BELOW: *Lou Gehrig congratulates Babe Ruth after his called shot homer.*

OPPOSITE: *Outfielder Babe Ruth of the Yankees in 1932*
BELOW: *Ruth leans on his bat during his last appearance with the Yankees – 13 June 1948.*

The Gashouse Gang Wins the 1935 Series

With Babe Ruth gone and the nation still in the midst of the Great Depression, the country and baseball needed another hero. They found both him and a whole team that reflected the toughness of the American people. The player was Jerome Herman 'Dizzy' Dean, and the team was the 'Gashouse Gang,' the St Louis Cardinals. In 1935 they became immortalized in a season and a World Series that went down in baseball history.

Dizzy Dean was one of the outstanding characters in baseball's Hall of Oddballs. Out of the hills of Arkansas, with a fastball that reminded the old timers of Walter Johnson, Dean became baseball's dominant pitcher. Wise-cracking and always smiling, Dizzy soon took the place of Ruth as baseball's favorite player. So confident was he of his ability that in one game against the Chicago Cubs Dean told the press before the game that he would only throw fastballs. The press made sure the Cubs knew it, but when it was over, Dizzy had thrown a three-hitter, shutting out an excellent Cubs team.

The year after Dizzy joined the Cardinals, they brought up his brother, Paul. The exact opposite of Dizzy, Paul was nevertheless hung with the nickname of 'Daffy.' And the younger Dean was quite a pitcher himself. In 1934 he threw a no-hitter at the Dodgers in the second game of a double-header.

Dizzy, taken aback by the attention the press was giving Paul, shouted, 'If I'da known Paul was gonna pitch a no-hitter, I'da done it too.' Dizzy had only thrown a three-hit shutout in the first game.

Dean wasn't the only character in the Gashouse Gang. They were all players who would do anything to win, and their dirt-stained uniforms proved it. Their manager was Frankie Frisch, The Fordham Flash. As a second baseman, he had few peers, and he was a lifetime .300 hitter. Although brash, argumentative and a fighter, the college-educated Frisch at first seemed out of place on the Gang, but he was one of them at heart, and they soon knew it.

Playing shortstop was Leo Durocher, he of the lip and chip on his shoulder. A fine fielder, Durocher often contributed the key hit to keep a rally going. At third was the 'Wild Horse of the Osage,' Pepper Martin, probably the best all-round third baseman in the league and more than probably the best base runner. And playing left field was Joe 'Ducky' Medwick, perhaps the heart of the Gashouse Gang. Day in and day out, Joe Medwick battled every pitcher on every pitch. A notori-

LEFT: *Frankie Frisch, 'The Fordham Flash,' the Manager of the 1934 Gashouse Gang.*
BOTTOM LEFT: *Dizzy Dean of the Cardinals and Schoolboy Rowe of the Tigers at the World Series.*
BELOW: *Joe 'Ducky' Medwick poses in front of the St Louis Cardinals dugout.*

ABOVE: *Paul 'Daffy' Dean won two games for the Cardinals in the 1934 Series.*
RIGHT: *Giant manager Bill Terry during his playing days.*

ous bad-ball hitter, his lifetime average was .324. A triple crown winner in 1937, Medwick was the most volatile member of the Gang.

In the 1935 National League pennant race the New York Giants were favored to win. And as late as mid-August they had an eight-game lead over the Cardinals and the rest of the league. The Giants' manager was Bill Terry, one of the few men to hit over .400 for a season. In spring training that year, Terry was asked by the press about various other teams in the league. When one scribe asked about the Brooklyn Dodgers, Terry sneered, 'Brooklyn? Are they still in the league?' Terry was to find out.

The Cardinals, behind the pitching of the Deans, came on strong, and going into the last two games of the season the Giants and the Cards were in a flat-footed tie. The Cards were playing the Cincinnati Reds, and the Giants were at home against – of all

teams – the Brooklyn Dodgers. And while Dizzy Dean was winning his 30th game of the season, the Dodgers beat the Giants. The next day, in front of thousands of Brooklyn fans at the Polo Grounds, the Dodgers completed the humiliation of the Giants, beating them again while the Cardinals were winning in St Louis.

A few weeks later, Casey Stengel, manager of the Dodgers, ran into Bill Terry at a dinner. Stengel told Terry that he had wanted to come over to the Giants dugout after that last game to offer best wishes. Terry, ever the diplomat, replied, 'It was good thing you didn't; I'da thrown your ass through the door!'

While the Cardinals had been chasing the Giants in the National League, the new superteam, the Detroit Tigers, easily replaced the Washington Senators as the kingpins of the American League. They had one of the best infields in baseball, with future Hall of Famers like Hank Greenberg at first and Charlie Gehringer at second. Proven pros Billy Rogell and Marv Owen rounded out the infield. As a team, the Tigers had a .300

average, and the pitching staff was excellent, headed by Lynwood (Schoolboy) Rowe, who won 24, and Tommy Bridges, who won 22. Their manager and catcher was Mickey Cochrane, the same Cochrane of Phila-delphia Athletics fame. The experts rated the Series a toss-up, and so it was, going into Game Seven at Detroit.

Although Dizzy Dean had pitched just two days earlier, Frisch named him his starter for the game. Dizzy wouldn't have let him name anyone else. The Tigers were delighted, having just beaten Dean. Thus far, the Series had been marred by threatened fights between the players, hard sliding and brush-back pitching. Judge Landis, Commissioner of Baseball, was so disturbed by the bad blood between the teams that he had come to Detroit to warn both teams to cool it.

The first two innings were scoreless, but there was such tension in the atmosphere that everyone knew it would not be long before there was an explosion. It came in the Cardinals' half of the third, and when the smoke settled this World Series was all but

over. It began quietly enough when Durocher flied out to center. Then Dizzy Dean doubled down the leftfield line. Next, Pepper Martin beat out an infield hit, with Dean going to third. Runners were now on first and third, but not for long, for Cochrane's old nemesis, Pepper Martin, promptly stole second. The frustrated Eldon Auker, pitching too carefully, walked Jack Rothrock. Frankie Frisch cleared the loaded bases with a double. Hoping to forestall the deluge, Coch-rane pulled starter Auker, replacing him with the hero of the Detroit staff, Schoolboy Rowe. Rowe got Medwick on a hard grounder to short, but Collins's single to left chased Frisch across, and when DeLancy double scored Collins, the Schoolboy was gone. His replacement, Elon Hogsett, gave up a single to Leo Durocher, loading the bases. Dizzy then scratch-ed a hit, and DeLancy scored, leaving the bases filled. When Hogsett, now shell-shocked by what was happening, walked Pepper Martin, he was pulled. Tommy Bridges came in and mercifully got Rothrock to bounce to Gehringer.

The inning had ended and so had the Tigers' hopes.

With a line-up of Greenberg, Gehringer, Cochrane and the rest, the Tigers probably had the talent to make a comeback against any pitcher except one. And that one was standing on the mound as Detroit came to bat in their half of the third. Dizzy Dean had had little trouble with the Tigers in the first two innings. Now he pulverized them. One Detroiter after another came to bat, heard the ball smack into the catcher's mitt and walked slowly back to the dugout. Inning after inning, Dizzy Dean showed the Tigers, their fans and the nation why he was the greatest pitcher in baseball.

In the sixth Pepper Martin got the Cardinals going again. He singled to left, and when the ball was mis-handled, Martin took off for second, easily beating the throw. Bridges got the next two Birds, but then Joe Med-wick tripled to deep right center field and slid hard into third ahead of the throw. As Tigers third baseman Marv Owen took the relay over the sliding Medwick, Medwick suddenly slashed upward with his left foot and the spikes just missed Owen's chest. Both benches erupted, and only the smart, quick work of the umpires stopped a full-scale brawl. Play was stopped for 20 minutes while the players milled around, shouting insults and threats to each other. Finally, the players returned to their benches, but the fans didn't stop booing.

When play finally resumed, the Cards still had Medwick on third. Collins promptly singled, and Medwick scored the ninth run of the Series. When the side was retired Medwick came out of the dugout and headed for his glove lying on the ground in left field. As he approached, the Tigers fans began throwing fruit and bottles at him. Medwick retreated to the infield while the umpires tried to quiet the fans. When they finally thought it was safe, they told Medwick to take his position, but as Joe trotted towards left field a torrent of oranges, liquor and pop bottles, seat cushions, and anything else throwable came cascading down from the bleachers. Medwick retreated again. After four such attempts, Judge Landis stood up in his box and signaled for the umpires to come over. Then he called Medwick and Owen and their managers, Frisch and Cochrane, over. After a brief conference Landis ordered Medwick to leave the field. Medwick, surrounded

by Detroit policemen, left through the Detroit dugout. A seat cushion sailed down from the grandstand and hit one of the policeman as Medwick disappeared into the runway.

Finally, the game continued, but it might as well have ended right there. Dean toyed with the Tigers, calling in what pitch he intended to throw and defying the Tigers to hit it. No matter that the Cardinals led 11-0; Dean was determined to throw a shut-out, and he did.

Dizzy Dean may have won the final

game of the 1934 World Series, but this game will live equally in baseball history as the great battle between Joe Medwick and the Tigers fans. Anyone who ever saw Joe Medwick play knows that no fans' anger could have kept him from playing. Only Judge Landis could have done that.

BELOW: *Dizzy Dean aids his own cause by scoring a run in the Series.*
BOTTOM: *Cardinal players amid debris thrown by disgruntled Detroit fans during the 1934 World Series.*

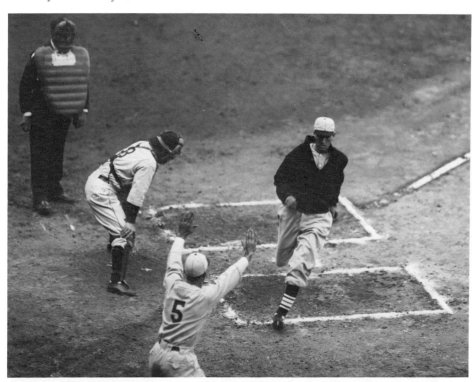

JOHNNY 'DOUBLE NO-HITTER' VANDER MEER

A no-hitter is a pitcher's dream. By 1938 there had been more than 50 no-hitters pitched in baseball, not counting games before there were two leagues. Some of baseball's greatest pitchers had pitched a no-hitter, and a few, like Cy Young and Christy Mathewson, had pitched no-hitters twice in their careers.

Sometimes pitchers will climb the heights and pitch a no-hitter, and then never be heard of again. But the no-hitter, whether pitched by an eventual Hall of Famer or a journeyman, is still a mark of greatness for a pitcher. Only once in baseball history has a pitcher ever pitched back-to-back no-hitters.

The Sporting News, baseball's bible of information, started a new feature in 1936. That year the editors began to name the persons who, in their opinion, were the outstanding players in a particular category, calling such individuals the game's 'No 1 Men of the Year.' In 1936, the Major League Player of the Year, according to *The Sporting News*, was Carl Hubble, the great pitcher of the New York Giants. *The Sporting News* named as Minor League Player of the Year one Johnny Vander Meer, a pitcher for the Durham club in the Piedmont League. (Durham was a farm club of the Cincinnati Reds.)

The Reds brought Vander Meer up to the big club in the spring of 1937, and everyone in the Cincinnati organization had high hopes that this outstanding prospect would be the answer to the Reds' problems. Their central problem was simply that they had a lousy team, and this was a problem beyond Vander Meer's powers to solve. He lasted only a few months before being sent down to Syracuse in the International League. Although possessed of a powerful build and outstanding athletic ability, Johnny Vander Meer broke the hearts of the Reds' fans, his manager and teammates because he was wild. He walked more batters than he struck out, and all the speed and power he had on his fastball was wasted when batter after batter would wait for him to walk them, which he usually did.

In the spring of 1938 Cincinnati management decided that they had to restructure Vander Meer's delivery. So they sent him back to Durham, not to the minor league team there, but to meet with another southpaw, Lefty Grove, of the Boston Red Sox. Grove himself had suffered from wildness when he came up to the big leagues in 1925 and joined Connie Mack's powerful Philadelphia Athletics. But Grove had cured his wildness and had gone on to become one of the greatest left-handed pitchers in modern baseball history. He won 300 games in a 17-year career and is today enshrined in Cooperstown.

Vander Meer was such a natural athlete that he had paid scant attention to the mechanics of pitching. When his control was on, he could strike out 15 batters in a game, but when it was off, he was terrible. Great pitchers know how to win even when their delivery isn't overpowering or their curve isn't working. Grove was like that. He talked to the young Vander Meer and explained to him such matters as the art of following through on each pitch. (He insisted, for example, that every time Johnny threw the ball he force

LEFT and RIGHT: *Left-hander Johnny Vander Meer of the Reds.*
BELOW: *The first night game ever at Ebbets Field in Brooklyn – 15 June 1938 – the scene of Vander Meer's second straight no-hitter.*

himself to follow through by making sure his left forearm hit his right knee.) By the time Vander Meer joined the Reds in spring training, he had spent most of his off season practicing the lessons that Lefty Grove had given him. And now the Johnny Vander Meer pitching for the Cincinnati Reds in the season of 1938 was finally living up to the ballyhoo about his natural talents.

On 11 June 1938 Johnny Vander Meer pitched against Boston, winning that game 3-0 and in so doing joining the select list of pitchers in baseball who had pitched a no-hitter. His next scheduled turn on the circuit was to be four days later, in Brooklyn, against the Dodgers.

The new owner of the Brooklyn Dodgers was Larry MacPhail. He had been general manager for the Cincinnati Reds when Vander Meer was signed, and his trades and deals had made a moribund franchise into a powerhouse by 1938. MacPhail was brash, inventive, tempestuous and a winner. Everyone in baseball hated him except the fans in the cities where he worked. In May 1935, after years of trying to convince the other seven owners of National League teams that night baseball could be good for the game, MacPhail and Reds owner Powell Crosley had joined 25,000-plus fans as President Roosevelt threw the switch in Washington, DC, that lit up Crosley Field for the first night game in major league baseball history.

Now, three years later, Larry MacPhail had brought night baseball to Brooklyn. What more fitting way to launch the idea in Brooklyn than to have as the opposition the team MacPhail had run when the first night game was played? And of course MacPhail knew that the famous Johnny Vander Meer was scheduled to pitch on 15 June, so he scheduled the inaugural night game for that date.

A record crowd of over 40,000 jammed Ebbets Field to see the spectacular that MacPhail had planned. Fireworks, bands, balloons and all were ready. MacPhail knew that Vander Meer had grown up across the Hudson River in the suburban town of Midland Park, NJ, so he made sure the pitcher's parents were in attendance, along with over 500 other fans from Vander Meer's home town. The novelty of night baseball and the chance to see Johnny Vander Meer made for a record attendance for a night game. In the end, the electric batteries that lit up the field were no match for the brilliance of Johnny Vander Meer.

For eight innings, Vander Meer allowed only one Dodger to reach second base, throwing back-to-back walks in the seventh. A four-run outburst by his teammates had given Vander Meer all the runs he would need. His fastball was a blur, and his curve was cracking down and hard. The Brooklyn batters couldn't even get a loud foul. By now all the fans knew they were watching a pitcher trying to accomplish something that had never happened in the history of the game. With each pitch, everyone in the park was rooting for Vandy.

After the Reds had their three at bats, Vander Meer strode to the mound to face the Dodgers in the last of the ninth. He easily got Buddy Hassett as he fielded Hassett's tap back to him in front of the mound and tagged Hassett out. But immortality isn't that easy to come by. Suddenly Vander Meer's control vanished, and that wicked fastball was just a ball. He walked Babe Phelps, Cookie Lavagetto and Dolph Camilli to load up the bases. With only one out and the bases loaded, Vander Meer now faced Ernie Koy. Koy hit a sharp bouncer to third baseman Lew Riggs, who was so careful with his throw to catcher Ernie Lombardi at home that there was no chance for a double play. Now Johnny Vander Meer had only one man to get out. Into the batters' box stepped Leo Durocher, an unpredictable hitter, just the kind who often breaks up no-hitters. On Vander Meer's first pitch, Durocher lined a hard drive down the leftfield line. As 40,000 people gasped, the ball curved foul. Now the left-hander threw his high, hard one. Durocher just got his bat on it, and the ball sailed lazily out to short center field. Harry Craft waited silently, as did the massed stands. When he caught it, Ebbets Field exploded, and thousands jumped the guard rails to rush to Vander Meer. Luckily for Johnny, his teammates got there first and rushed him to the Reds' dugout.

Very few baseball fans remember that night baseball came to Brooklyn on 15 June 1938, but they all remember that Johnny Vander Meer achieved immortality that night.

DI MAGGIO'S 56 STRAIGHT

As baseball entered the fourth decade of its modern era some of the greatest players who would ever play the game were performing. The 1940 season opened with Bob Feller pitching an opening day no-hitter against the Chicago White Sox. That season Feller won 27 games, and he won 25 more in 1941, before joining the United States Navy. Hank Greenberg was starring for the Detroit Tigers, and Mel Ott and

RIGHT: *Joe DiMaggio, the Hall of Fame outfielder of the Yankees, warms up.*
BELOW: *DiMaggio takes a cut in a game with the Washington Senators.*

Carl Hubble still led the New York Giants. Leo Durocher had taken over as manager of the Brooklyn Dodgers, and he had a host of stars, led by Pete Reiser, called by Branch Rickey 'the greatest ball player I ever saw.' Enos Slaughter and Marty Marrion led the Cardinals, and a slim, quiet rookie from Donora, Pennsylvania, with a funny stance joined the Cardinals. His name was Stan Musial, and everyone agreed he'd never make it in the biggies with that stance. How wrong they were.

In terms of individual achievement, the baseball season of 1941 will never be surpassed. The reason is simple. Among all the great players there were two who were at the peak of their careers, and if nothing else had happened, they alone would have made 1941 the most memorable year in baseball history. Their names were Joe DiMaggio and Ted Williams.

In 1933, the most sought-after minor league player in baseball had been a 19-year-old centerfielder for the San Francisco Seals. Offers in excess of $100,000 were offered the Seals for Joe DiMaggio, but they declined, reasoning that his value would increase in 1934. DiMaggio had given baseball a

hint of what was to come when he hit in 61 straight games. But in 1934, while getting out of a cab, Joe DiMaggio suffered a knee injury and sat out much of the season. His injury made him suspect, and the offers for his contract dried up. Finally, the Yankees agreed to pay $25,000, plus a handful of minor leaguers, to the California team, and Di Maggio became their property. He played his first season with them in 1936. Blessed with speed, power and grace, Joe DiMaggio quickly became the dominant player in the American League. By 1941 DiMaggio was such a famous figure that a song had been written about him, and while no gold record, 'Joltin' Joe DiMaggio' was a solid hit.

With DiMaggio joining Lou Gehrig, Bill Dickey, Frank Crosetti and Red Rolfe, the Yankees won four consecutive World Series from 1936-1939. While Babe Ruth and his gargantuan home runs had been the symbol of the Yankees in the Twenties and early Thirties, DiMaggio's cool, businesslike efficiency now became the hallmark of the new Yankees. Almost effortless in his fielding, base running and hitting, DiMaggio was certainly one of the most complete players ever to play the game.

The Yankees made quick work of the pennant race in 1941. Upset by their third-place finish in 1940, Manager Joe McCarthy made sure this team took the race seriously. In addition to Di-Maggio, Dickey and Rolfe, McCarthy had Tommy Henrich, Charlie Keller, Joe Gordon and rookie shortstop Phil Rizzuto. It was another great team.

Early in May 1941 DiMaggio was in a slump, hitting only .306. Bob Feller had held him hitless in his last game, and when the Yankees opened up against the White Sox in New York, little attention was paid when DiMaggio finally got a hit off Edgar Smith. He hit safely in the next 10 games, and then the next ten, and when he had hit safely in 29 straight games, the newspapers began to check on who held what records for consecutive hitting streaks. Rogers Hornsby had hit in 33 straight games, the National League record. George Sisler held the modern record of 41, set in 1922, the same year Hornsby set his, and the all-time record was 44, set by Willie Keeler of Baltimore in 1897.

On 21 June Joltin' Joe singled off Dizzy Trout of Detroit, and he passed Hornsby. By now, DiMaggio's streak was making headlines in every sports page in the country. Fans flocked to fill the arenas wherever the Yankees played. In a doubleheader at Griffith Stadium in Washington, a sellout crowd saw DiMaggio double off of Dutch Leonard and equal the record of George Sisler. In the second game, Joe discovered that his favorite bat had been stolen during the intermission. He was retired on his first three times at bat, and as he went to the on-deck circle to bat for the fourth and probably final time, Tommy Henrich offered the Jolter his own bat. Joe accepted, and on the second pitch from Red Anderson, he lined a base hit, and he had the modern record. On 2 July when Joe homered off Dick Newsome of the Boston Red Sox, he broke Willie Keeler's record. Now the only question was when it would end.

The streak was at 56 games when the Yankees played Cleveland in Munici-pal Stadium. Over 70,000 fans jammed the old ballpark on the shores of Lake Erie. From the time that the streak had started on 14 May the Yankee Clipper had come to bat 223 time and had

batted .408, with 92 hits, 15 home runs and 55 runs batted in. Now, in his first at bat, Joe lashed a drive down the left-field line. It looked like a sure hit, but Kenny Keltner of the Indians dove to his left, backhanded the drive and threw Joe out at first. He walked in the fourth inning, and in the seventh, his sharp hit was speared by the same Keltner. With the Yankees leading 4-3, DiMaggio came to bat in the top of the eighth against reliever Jim Bagby. He took a strike from Bagby, then drove the ball hard towards the hole at second base. But shortstop Lou Boudreau raced over, picked up the ball, flipped to second for the force, whence it went on to first to complete the double play.

So it was over. Joe DiMaggio's streak of hitting in consecutive games ended at 56. And many baseball experts today still think that this is another indivi-dual record that will never be broken. The next day, DiMaggio started an-other streak that lasted 16 games. In the course of 73 games, he had hit safely in 72 of them. Perhaps only two brilliant plays by Kenny Keltner had prevented Yankee Clipper's record from being 73 straight.

LEFT: *Frank Crosetti, the all-star infielder for the New York Yankees.*
BELOW: *DiMaggio was hailed by his teammates after setting the consecutive games hitting record.*

TED HITS .406

He was first and always 'The Kid.' The first day he arrived at the Boston Red Sox spring training camp in Bradenton, Florida, the equipment man looked up and saw a gangly, mop-headed 19-year-old. 'Hey kid,' he called, 'you're late. Put these on and get out on the field.' So Ted Williams came to the Boston Red Sox, and his reception by the veterans wasn't what he had hoped for. They had all heard about him, but since he was trying to take one of their jobs, they rode him unmercifully. 'Hey kid, do this' and 'Hey kid, don't you know anything?'

When spring training was over, he saw his name on the list of players to be sent to the minors. When he saw some

BELOW: *Theodore Samuel Williams, 'The Splendid Splinter,' at the plate.*

of the veterans laughing at him, he hollered, 'I'll be back you SOBs, and I'll make more money than all of you put together.' Later he asked the equipment man how much they really did make, and when he was told $15,000 each, he gulped and borrowed $5 to take the bus to Minneapolis.

Unlike Joe DiMaggio, when Ted Williams was starting out in minor league ball in San Diego, there were no 'can't miss' signs on him. In fact, when Tris Speaker, the Hall of Famer who worked in the front office of the Boston Red Sox, was sent west to scout a San Diego player, the player he was to scout was Bobby Doerr. But when he saw Ted Williams hit, Speaker wasted no time in signing both players. One night, after playing a game in San Francisco, Williams was introduced to Lefty O'Dool, a former major leaguer and one of the city's more celebrated saloon keepers. Williams asked O'Dool what he had to do to become a great hitter, and O'Dool replied, 'Never let them change your swing, kid.'

By the Fall of 1941 DiMaggio's streak was history, and the Yankees had such a huge lead that the only interest left in the American League was following Ted Williams in his unlikely pursuit of the hitters' ultimate goal, a .400 season. The last time it had happened was in 1931, but now, almost before anyone quite realized it, Williams was approaching Bill Terry's 10-year-old record.

The last day of the season found the Red Sox visiting the Philadelphia Athletics at Shibe Park. Williams's batting average going into the scheduled doubleheader was .39955. When rounded off, that produced .400,

and across the country press and fans alike debated whether Ted should play on Sunday or sit it out and assure himself of hitting .400. The sentiment in the press was that he should sit it out; the fans wanted him to play.

In the Red Sox locker room before the game Joe Cronin, manager of the Bosox, asks Williams if he wants to play. 'It's up to you,' says Cronin. 'Do you want to play or sit it out?' 'I'll play,' answers Williams without hesitation.

Over 10,000 people have come out on this cold, damp, dreary Sunday in Philadelphia. The line-up cards are handed by the umpires to the public address announcer, and when he says, 'Batting third and playing left field for Boston: Williams,' the crowd roars, and the rest of the names are lost in the tumult.

On his first at bat, Williams singles sharply off Dick Fowler. The next time up, with Fowler still pitching, the Kid slams a home run to dead center field. Now, if he can just walk or get another hit, the .400 season is assured. Connie Mack, manager of the Athletics, doesn't want his team to go down in the books as the one that let Ted Williams break .400, so he pulls the ineffective Fowler and brings in a lefty, Porter Vaughan. Williams smashes such a single through the box that, had it hit Vaughan, the pitcher's career might have been over. Three for three, and in the seventh he gets his fourth

---

TOP RIGHT: *Williams played left field for his entire 19-year career with the Boston Red Sox.*
BELOW: *Ted Williams was twice named the American League's Most Valuable Player — in 1946 and 1949.*

hit, another single to right. On his last at bat in the first game, Ted Williams walks, and his batting average is now .404. He has done it, and as the game ends the Philadelphia fans stand and cheer Williams as he heads for the dugout.

Everyone knows that Williams will sit out the second game. After all, he has proven his mettle by playing in the first game, when he was assured of a .400 season if he sat on the bench. But when the public address announcer gets to the third name in the Red Sox lineup, he again says, 'And Ted Williams batting third,' and the crowd stands anew to show their appreciation for this remarkable hitter. In Game Two, Williams has a single and a double in three at bats. The double smashes the public address speaker in right field. When the final statistics are published at the end of the game, Ted Williams's batting average for the 1941 season is .4057 or, rounded off, .406!

The Kid would go on to compile records as a hitter that few have ever attained, even though he would lose five complete seasons in the service of his country in World War II and in the Korean War. Had Ted Williams played in those seasons, three of which he missed while in his early twenties, there is no question that his records would be the ones today's players would chase. But statistics were not what made Ted Williams one of the most admired hitters of his time. To see Ted Williams at bat was to watch a consummate artist, a once-in-a-lifetime hitter. Back when he was just a rookie, he was asked what he wanted to be in baseball. Williams replied, 'I want to be remembered as the greatest hitter who ever lived.' Many people remember him just that way.

As if the 1941 seaon were not already the most memorable in baseball history because of Ted Williams's .406 average and Joe DiMaggio's 56-game hitting streak, it ended in one of the greatest of great Series.

For years, 23 of them, the Brooklyn Dodgers were almost always somewhere at the bottom of the standings when the season ended. To be sure, Bill Terry's sarcastic query about whether the Dodgers were 'still in the league' may have cost him and his Giants the 1934 National League pennant, but apart from that triumph, the Brooklyn faithful could only say, 'Wait 'til next year.'

Living in the same city that had the New York Yankees and the New York Giants, the Dodgers were always low men on the totem pole of New York baseball. Seldom did they have a great player, and when they did come up with a star he was usually part clown, like Casey Stengel or Babe Herman, and seemed small beer when compared to the headliners of the efficient Yankees or the powerful Giants. But in 1938 the Dodgers brought Larry Mac-Phail in from Cincinnati to be their

'HOW COME, MICK?'

general manager, and in three years the Dodgers were the champions of the National League. First, MacPhail bought the great Joe Medwick from the Cardinals. Then, when Judge Landis ruled that the Cardinals had a monopoly on young talent and forced them to break up their farm system, Mac-Phail got Pete Reiser from the Redbirds, and a potential Hall of Famer was wearing the Brooklyn blue. In addition to Medwick and the gifted Reiser, MacPhail also picked up Mickey Owen from the Cardinals.

Then he picked Pee Wee Reese out of the Red Sox farm system, and the Dodgers had their shortstop for the next 15 years. Second baseman Billy Herman came over from the Cubs, and Dolph Camilli and Kirby Higbe from the Phillies. Add Whit Wyatt and Dixie Walker, 'the people's cherse,' and you have a team that could play with the best in baseball. When MacPhail put Leo Durocher in charge as manager, the flashy, quick-witted, tart-tongued Durocher quickly put the final stamp on this tough, exciting team.

The Dodgers didn't back down from anyone, and soon there were so many brawls between them and the other teams in the National League that Judge Landis had to warn MacPhail and Durocher. Naturally, the fans of the Yankees and the Giants looked down their noses at such behavior, but to the long-suffering Brooklyn fans these 'Bums' were their pride and joy. When the Dodgers clinched the National League pennant, Brooklyn went wild, and the fact that the hated, haughty Yankees were their opponents made it all the more intoxicating. All of Brooklyn made ready for war.

ABOVE: *Pete Reiser scores after hitting a home run in the 1941 World Series.*
LEFT: *Third baseman Harry 'Cookie' Lavagetto of the Dodgers slides in to score in the first game.*

ABOVE: *Tommy Henrich is out at second as Billy Herman throws to first to complete the double play.*
BOTTOM: *Catcher Mickey Owen goes after the passed ball in the fourth game.*

The opening game, in the Bronx, was a great pitching duel, Red Ruffing beating Curt Davis as the Yankees won 3-2. Next, Brooklyn returned the favor, winning 3-2. The Series then moved to Brooklyn for the next three games. In Game Three, the Yankees won 2-1 as Marius Russo overshadowed Hugh Casey, the best relief pitcher in the National League.

Game Four. The Dodgers knew they must win, and they waited impatiently while Mayor Fiorello LaGuardia posed for pictures before throwing out the ceremonial first ball. The day was exceptionally hot for October, and the players were sweating freely in their woolen uniforms. The Yankees drew first blood, scoring in the first and fourth innings to lead 3-0. But the Dodgers got two back in their half of the fourth and went ahead 4-3 when Pete Reiser, the National League's leading hitter, whacked a home run with Dixie Walker on second. The Dodgers now had the momentum, and

with Hugh Casey pitching in relief, the Brooklyn faithful smelled victory. Casey had come on in the fifth inning, with the bases loaded with Yankees and had retired the side with no damage.

Through the rest of the innings, the Yankees were helpless against Casey, and although the Dodgers didn't score, they seemed to be in command. In the first of the ninth, Casey easily disposed of the Yankees' first two hitters, Strum and Rolfe. Now, with one out to go, he would have to work carefully against the dangerous Tommy Henrich. The count went to three and two. Casey

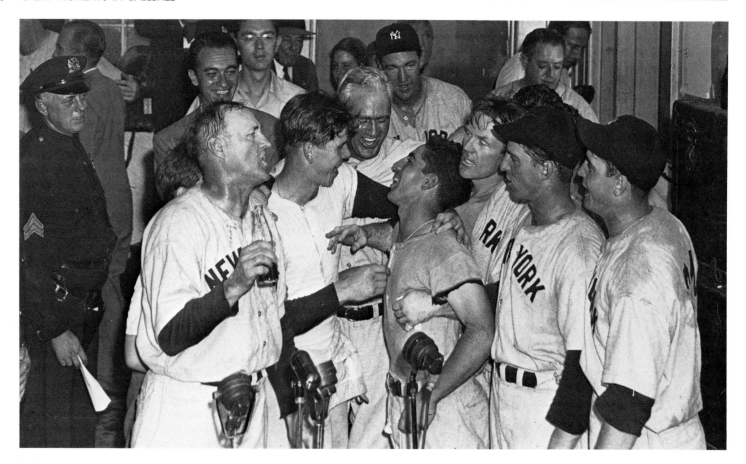

snapped off a sharp-breaking curve. Henrich swung and missed, and the Dodgers and their fans started for the mound.

But they have hardly begun to move when they see that catcher Mickey Owen has dropped the third strike. The ball rolls over towards the Dodgers dugout, with Owen in mad chase. Henrich, who had thrown down his bat in disgust, sees Owen running, and he takes off for first. By the time Owen recovers the missed strike, Henrich is safe. The silence in Ebbets Field is broken only by the groans of the stunned faithful. But even though Owen has allowed a passed ball, the Dodgers still lead, and there are two out.

Coming to bat is Joe DiMaggio, and he quickly slams Casey's pitch to left field for a clean single. Next up is Charlie Keller, with men on first and second and two out. Casey is obviously shaken and looks around for help. Oddly, Durocher doesn't come out to calm down his pitcher, and none of the Dodgers infielders comes to the mound to say a word of encouragement.

Casey gets two quick strikes on Keller, and with the crowd praying for him, Casey grooves the 0-2 pitch. Keller swings, and the ball shoots out towards the rightfield bleachers. On the crack of the bat, Henrich and DiMaggio take off for home. The ball, hit so hard by Keller that it doesn't even rise, smacks into the top of the rightfield fence, and Keller, not the

swiftest of the Yankees, stands on second with a double. Still Durocher makes no move to help the struggling Casey.

TOP: *The Yankees celebrate the winning of the 1941 World Series.*
BELOW: *Mickey Owen, the Dodger catcher and the goat of the Series.*

The Dodgers now trail 5-4, Keller is on second and Bill Dickey comes to bat. Casey walks him, and still Durocher does nothing. Curt Davis is warming up for the Dodgers as fast as he can, but nobody is calling time out and going to the mound. Now the batter is Joe Gordon, an excellent hitter. Again Casey gets two strikes, only to have Gordon smash a fastball to the leftfield corner and send Keller and Dickey home. Mercifully, Rizzuto grounds out and the debacle is over. The Yankees lead 7-4, and the Dodgers go down meekly in the last of the ninth, three up and three down. The Dodgers and their fans know the World Series is over, even though there will be a fifth game tomorrow. As expected the Yankees win that and take the Series, four games to one.

What happened in Game Four is now remembered in baseball and World Series history for the Mickey Owen passed ball. But to some, there seemed to be another, graver error in the game. Durocher didn't protect Casey after the passed ball and let him pitch to DiMaggio and Keller. The result was that Casey grooved two pitches to Keller and Gordon that brought in four runs. Still, it was Owen who had to take the heat, who had to spend the rest of his life remembered as the man who missed Tommy Henrich's third strike, who, wherever he went, had to contend with the inevitable question, 'How come, Mick?'

Slaughter's Dash for Home

The year 1946 saw the world again at peace and struggling to bring order out of the chaos World War II had brought to mankind. For baseball, it was a return to normality – no more oldtimers in the big leagues, for the young men had come back. Stan Musial was the MVP in the National League, leading the league in hitting at .365, as well leading in hits, doubles, triples, slugging, runs and total bases. Bob Feller had won 26 games and set a new season strikeout record, with 338, and had 36 complete games, the most since Walter Johnson had 38 back in 1910. Ted Williams was named the American League's Most Valuable Player, batting .342, with 123 RBIs and 38 home runs. And to keep things almost the same as they had been in 1942, the Brooklyn Dodgers and the St Louis Cardinals battled down to the last day to decide who would represent the National League against the Boston Red Sox in the World Series. But this time the Cards and the Bums went 1942 one better: They finished in a flat-footed tie, each with identical records of 96-58. For the first time there was a best-two-out-of-three playoff for a pennant. The Cardinals won, two games to zero, and captured their fourth pennant in five years.

The Boston Red Sox had easily won the American League pennant over the Yankees, and writers were describing their team as one of the greatest. Led by Williams, there were All Stars at most positions. Bobby Doerr and Johnny Pesky not only formed the best double play combination in the league, but hit powerfully. Rudy York, at first base, was a home run hitter. Dom DiMaggio, Joe's brother, played center field, and many said he was the equal of his brother when it came to fielding his position. The fine pitching staff featured Tex Hughson and Boo Ferris.

For the Cardinals, 1946 brought back their great outfield of Stan Musial, Enos Slaughter and Terry Moore. Marty Marrion was the premier shortstop in the National League, and his sidekick at second base was Red Schoendienst. Whitey Kurowski was at the hot corner, and manager Eddie

Outfielder Enos 'Country' Slaughter scores in the 1946 World Series.

Dyer had recently moved Musial to first base so that Harry 'The Hat' Walker could play in the field. A fine hitter, Walker was a student of hitting, and in 1947 he would replace Musial as the National League batting champion. The Cardinals' pitching staff had Johnny Beazley and Howie Pollet back, but the new ace of the staff was Harry 'The Cat' Brecheen, who had won the last playoff game against the Dodgers.

The Red Sox were favored in this Series because it was thought that the Cardinals had worn out their pitching staff in the bitter pennant race with the Dodgers. Enos Slaughter had a bad arm, and there were other injuries, whereas the Red Sox had a fully rested staff and no injuries.

The teams opened in St Louis, and the favored Beantowners beat Howie Pollet and the Cardinals 3-2. Behind

Brecheen, the Cardinals evened the series 3-0. Game Three in Boston went to the Red Sox 4-0, as Boo Ferris shut out the Redbirds. This 'you win one and I'll win the next' routine continued as the Cardinals next slugged the Bosox 12-3, and then Boston won Game Five 6-3. Back in St Louis, Harry Brecheen won his second game 4-1, and the Series was tied up at three victories each.

For the last game, Manager Eddie Dyer picked Murry Dickson to pitch for the Cardinals. The Red Sox countered with Boo Harris. The Cardinals took a 3-1 lead into the eighth inning, but then the Red Sox began to get to Dickson. After two hits by the Sox, Dyer sent in Harry Brecheen. As The Cat came to the mound from the bullpen, many wondered if he had anything left after his brilliant seven-hit performance in Game Six. With two men on and nobody out, Brecheen fanned Wally Moses. Next came the dangerous Pesky. He smashed a liner to right, but

LEFT: *Harry 'The Cat' Brecheen, the star lefty of the St Louis Cardinals in 1946.*
BELOW: *Dom DiMaggio is forced out at home by Cardinal catcher Joe Garagiola.*

Enos Slaughter grabbed it, and even though the Red Sox knew Slaughter had a bad arm, no one dared try to advance. Still runners on second and third, and now two outs. But Dom DiMaggio was more than just a great fielder. He could hit, and did so, tying the score at 3-3.

In the Cardinals' eighth, Enos Slaughter opened with a single. Whitey Kurowski and Del Rice failed to hit, and Harry Walker stepped up. Slaughter led away from first, and Manager Dyer signaled for the hit-and-run, hoping a hit would get Slaughter to third. Walker knocked a soft drive to left field, and Slaughter was already half way to second when the ball bounced between Williams and DiMaggio. Johnny Pesky was running towards left to get the cut-off throw and, with his back to the infield, couldn't hear his infield teammates yelling to him. They were seeing Slaughter rounding third and running right through the coach's stop signal.

Pesky caught the cut-off throw and wheeled back towards home, only to find Slaughter racing down the third base line. The stunned Pesky hesitated a split second and then threw to catcher Hal Wagner. But 'Country' Slaughter was already sliding home safely by the time Wagner got Pesky's throw. Now the Cardinals led 4-3.

In the ninth Brecheen, pitching with only one day's rest and running a fever, gave up opening hits to Rudy York and Bobby Doerr. But then he got Higgins to hit into a force of Doerr at third and Roy Partee to pop up; and when pinch-hitter Tom McBride forced Higgins at second, the St Louis Cardinals were World Champions for the third time in five years.

Slaughter's mad dash for home won the Series for the Redbirds, and Harry Brecheen won his third World Series game. It had been 26 years since a pitcher accomplished that feat. But if Slaughter's run and Brecheen's pitching were the highlights of the final

Slaughter, Brecheen, Dyer and Walker celebrate the World Series victory of the Cardinals.

game, it was Harry 'The Hat' Walker who was the hitting star of the Series. Another hitting star for the Cardinals was catcher Joe Garagiola, who hit a phenomenal .383.

Hours after the Red Sox club house had been cleaned up, and most of the press and players had departed, a solitary figure sat on a stool in front of his locker. Ted Williams h'ad suffered through his most embarrassing seven days in baseball. He had hit just .200. All his hits were singles, he had struck out five times and he had driven in just one run. He would go on to become for many the greatest hitter in baseball history, but he would never again have the chance to play in a World Series. And the Boston press, never fond of the 'Splendid Splinter,' would never let Williams forget his poor showing in the 'Series Slaughter Stole.'

THE DODGERS SIGN JACKIE ROBINSON

special person, and Rickey picked him not only for his natural talent, but also for his intelligence and self-control. As a ballplayer, Jackie Robinson was the hub of Dodgers teams that would dominate the National League for a decade.

In a sense, Rickey's action was self-serving, for he was after all adding a stellar new player to the Dodgers' roster, a player whose performance

On 11 April 1947 Branch Rickey dragged the national pastime kicking and screaming into the mainstream of social reform. Since 1942 the owner of the Brooklyn Dodgers had quietly planned to break the unwritten law baseball had inflicted on itself: that blacks could not play baseball with whites.

Rickey, a serious, honorable man, had long been troubled by the inequities in American society. When President Harry Truman signed an executive order integrating the Armed Forces of the United States, Rickey knew the time was ripe. Rickey also was a great baseball man and knew that there was a vast untapped source of talent in the black leagues. He had been quietly scouting, and the reports he had received told him of an exceptional young second baseman with the Kansas City Monarchs of the Negro American League.

That was in 1942, and when Jackie Robinson returned from the war, along with millions of other American fighting men, Rickey signed him to a contract with the Montréal Royals, the Dodgers' top farm club in the International League. Robinson led the league in hitting and stolen bases, and everyone in baseball knew that Rickey was going to buy his contract. He did, and on 12 April 1947 Jackie Robinson reported to the Brooklyn Dodgers'

spring training camp in Vero Beach, Florida.

Millions of words have been written about Jackie Robinson and what he had to overcome as the first of his race to play in the majors. Robinson was a

ABOVE: *Jackie Robinson when he was with the Montréal Royals.*
BOTTOM LEFT: *Branch Rickey (right) shakes hands with Jackie Robinson.*

could be expected to pay off in games won and rising gate receipts. But to show how genuine Rickey's concern was for integrating baseball, he deliberately refrained from signing Larry Doby because Bill Veech, another enlightened baseball man who owned the Cleveland Indians, also wanted to sign Doby. Rickey knew it was important that the American League also begin integrating, so he told Veech to go ahead and sign Doby, who thus became the American League's first black player. In 12 more years every major league team would have at least one black player.

In 1942, when Rickey began scouting the black leagues, *The Sporting News*, baseball's 'bible,' was still steadfast in its opposition to admitting blacks to the majors. In 1947 *The Sporting News* voted for Jackie Robinson as 'Rookie of the Year.'

THE YANKEES WIN THE 1947 SERIES

By 1947 the Yankees had returned to their accustomed place as champions of the American League, and once again they would face the Dodgers in the Series. The Brooklyn faithful had been waiting since 1941 to see their beloved Bums erase the humiliation of Mickey Owen's dropped third strike. The 1947 World Series would live up to everyone's expectations.

The Yankees won the first two games easily behind Speck Shea and Allie Reynolds, 5-3 and 10-3. But back home in Ebbets Field, the Dodgers squeaked through to win 9-8. A rookie catcher for the Yankees, Larry Berra, had hit a pinch-hit homer, but Hugh Casey held on for the Dodgers' first win in the Series.

In the history of the fall classic, no pitcher had ever pitched a no-hitter. Interestingly, two Chicago Cubs pitchers had come the closest, Ed Reulbach in 1906 and Claude Passeau in 1945: Each had a one-hitter. On 3 October 1947 Bill Bevens of the New York Yankees took the mound against the Dodgers in Game Four. For eight and two thirds innings, Floyd (Bill) Bevens held the Brooklyn Dodgers hitless.

A big, strong pitcher, Bevens had a good fastball and curve, but he had problems with his control. In this game, even though he had held the Dodgers hitless, he led only 2-1 going into the ninth. (Bevens had walked in a run in the fifth inning.) Both Tommy Henrich and Joe DiMaggio had made great fielding plays to keep Bevens's no-hitter going, but by the ninth Bevens had walked eight Yankees, one short of the World Series record. Johnny Lindell kept the no-hitter alive when he made a leaping catch of Bruce Edwards's long drive deep in left field, but then Bevens walked Carl Furillo to

TOP RIGHT: *Allie Pierce 'Superchief' Reynolds, the pitching ace of the New York Yankees.*
RIGHT: *Right-handed pitcher Bill Bevens of the New York Yankees.*

tie the record he *didn't* want. The Dodgers' Spider Jorgensen next popped out to the first baseman, George McQuinn, and Burt Shotton, the Dodgers' manager, sent in speedy Al Gionfriddo to run for Furillo.

Bevens now faced Pete Reiser, a Reiser who was a shadow of the great player he once was. Reiser had suffered so many injuries that, even though still a young man, his power and speed had been greatly reduced. But he was still not a man to be taken lightly.

Bevens, with the count of two balls and one strike on Reiser, took a little too long with the next pitch, and on a signal from Shotton, Gionfriddo stole second. Now Yankees manager Bucky Harris ordered Bevens to intentionally walk Reiser, thereby violating one of the cardinal rules of managing: Never put the lead run on base. Bevens did as he was told, and now he owned the record for most walks in a World Series game, ten.

Shotton now ordered a pinch-hitter for Eddie Stankey, the veteran Cookie Lavagetto, and sent in Eddie Miksis to run for the infirm Reiser. Lavagetto took a hard swing at Bevens's first pitch and missed. But he smashed the next pitch hard towards the rightfield wall. Gionfriddo and Miksis were off and running with the crack of the bat. Tommy Henrich, who had already saved Bevens with a great catch earlier, raced towards the ball and the wall. Lavagetto's hit landed high on the wall and bounced down towards the running Henrich, who had to scoop it up

ABOVE: *Cookie Lavagetto bats in the winning run of the fourth game.*
BELOW: *Joe Page, the southpaw fireman of the Yankee pitching staff.*

and fire it to McQuinn, the cut-off man. McQuinn wheeled and fired to Berra at home plate. But it was too late: Both Gionfriddo and Miksis crossed the plate ahead of the relay.

Lavagetto was mobbed by the Dodgers, and their fans went crazy in the stands and on the field. Bill Bevens quietly walked off the field into the Yankees dugout, stunned and beaten. He had given only one hit to the Dodgers, but the walks had finally caught

up with him. Cookie Lavagetto was the toast of Brooklyn and would long be remembered in Brooklyn Dodgers history. But Bill Bevens would be remembered as the pitcher who walked himself out of immortality.

The Yankees won Game Five 2-1. In Game Six, little Al Gionfriddo made a catch that saved the game for the Dodgers. Leading 8-5, Burt Shotton, the Dodgers' manager, had inserted the speedy Gionfriddo for defensive purposes into left field. With two men on, Joe DiMaggio came to bat. He had had a tough series at bat, but his fielding had been as flawless as ever. Now the Yankee Clipper drove the ball deep into left field at Yankee Stadium, and it seemed that the Yankees were about to tie the game. But Gionfriddo turned and dashed back towards the fence, 405 feet from home. When he got to the fence, he turned and picked off the DiMaggio drive just as it crossed the fence. The Yankees fans were stunned, and even the usually phlegmatic DiMaggio was seen kicking the dirt between first and second base after Gionfriddo's great catch. Thus the Dodgers got out of the inning and held on to win Game Six 8-6.

In Game Seven the Yankees won 5-2 behind the five-inning relief pitching of Joe Page. The Dodgers had certainly come up with the more memorable moments in the Series, but in the end it was the New York Yankees who prevailed. Once again the Brooklyn Dodgers and their fans would have to wait 'til next year.

The Phillies win the National League Flag

In 1950 a rematch between the Dodgers and Yankees was planned by most of the nation's baseball writers. Both teams seemed strong, and the Dodgers, in particular, seemed set. But along came a Philadelphia team nicknamed the 'Whiz Kids' and spoiled the experts' forecast. Going into the last game of the season, the winner of the game between the Dodgers and Phillies at Ebbets Field would decide who would represent the National League against the Yankess.

The star of the Phillies was a strong-armed right-handed pitcher from Michigan State University named Robin Roberts. Pitching for the Dodgers was their strong rookie, Don Newcombe.

In a fierce pitching duel, Roberts and the Phillies led 1-0 going into the bottom of the sixth. Pee Wee Reese, the Dodgers' light-hitting shortstop, hit a high fly to right. Reese saw the ball come down and bounce back up as it hit the top of the high rightfield wall. Thinking the ball was in play, Reese raced around the bases and slid into third. The crowd roared with laughter because, unlike Reese, they knew the ball had bounced over the fence for a homer.

RIGHT: *Robin Roberts, the star right-handed pitcher of the 1950 Philadelphia Phillies.*
BELOW: *Willie Jones, Del Ennis, Andy Seminick and Dick Sisler – the Whiz Kids' Murderers' Row.*

In the Dodgers' ninth, with the score tied at one, Cal Abrams led off with a walk from Roberts. Reese twice tried to bunt Abrams to second and failed, so he singled to center, with Abrams stopping at second. Now Duke Snider came to bat, and everyone knew he'd bunt to get Abrams to third and Reese to second. But the Duke crossed up the experts and lined a sharp single to center. Richie Ashburn raced in from center and in one quick move picked up Snider's hit and fired the ball home to catcher Stan Lopatta. Ashburn's throw was right on target and Abrams, rounding third, couldn't stop in time and was tagged out. But Reese and Snider had advanced, so the Dodgers still had runners on second and third and only one out. Jackie Robinson was intentionally walked to fill the bases, and when Carl Furillo swung and topped the ball, the Phillies had two out. But now the Dodgers' leading home run hitter, Gil Hodges, came to bat. Hodges hit a long drive to the

deepest part of Ebbets Field, but Del Ennis of the Phillies caught the ball right in front of the scoreboard. No runs for the Bums.

In their tenth, Roberts is the Phil's first batter and he wraps a single to center. Eddie Watkus then pops a short single to center, and Roberts stops at second. Richie Ashburn, the Phillies' leading hitter and a good bunter, is up, and he bunts Newcombe's first pitch. But Newcombe is quick, and he fields the bunt and throws to third for the force on Roberts. Now coming to bat is Dick Sisler, who already has three singles off Newcombe. (Sisler's father is George Sisler, a Hall of Fame member and an employee of the Brooklyn Dodgers.) Sisler swings at the first pitch and misses. He fouls off the second. But he gets all of Newcombe's next pitch, driving it over the 348-ft mark in left field. A three-run homer; and now the Phillies lead 4-1. In their half of the ninth, the Dodgers can't do anything against the pitching of

ABOVE: *Dick Sisler is mobbed after hitting the homer that won the 1950 World Series.*

Roberts, and as he retires the side the Phillies break from the dugout to mob their pitcher. For the first time since 1915, a wait of 35 years, the Philadelphia Phillies, the 'Whiz Kids,' are champions of the National League.

They were called the 'Whiz Kids' because of the youthfulness of their stars, Roberts, Ashburn, Ennis and Curt Simmons. But the team had no World Series experience, and to add to their difficulties, stirrings in an Asian nation called Korea suddenly obliged Curt Simmons, their left-handed ace, to go off on military service. Without Simmons, and lacking the Yankees' overwhelming power and experience, the Phillies were swept in the Series in four games. No one was really surprised by this, and no one really felt that it diminished the glory the 'Whiz Kids' had won in their dazzling championship season.

FELLER THROWS HIS THIRD NO-HITTER

Since his arrival as a 17-year-old wunderkind in 1936, the Cleveland Indians' Bob Feller had been the outstanding pitcher of his time. A flame-throwing right-hander, Feller consistently won 20 games a season and struck out over 300 batters, and in 1946, he struck out 348 batters. (To put this accomplishment in perspective, consider that only one other pitcher in the league struck out more than 200 hitters, and only nine others registered over 100 strikeouts.) Feller pitched his first no-hitter against the Chicago White Sox on Opening Day in 1940. This went into the record books because no pitcher before or since has had an Opening Day no-hitter. He got his second in April 1946 against the New York Yankees. And on 1 July 1951 Bob Feller threw his third no-hitter against the Detroit Tigers. No pitcher in modern baseball has thrown three no-hitters in his career.

Ironically, by the 1951 season many experts had thought Feller was over the hill. He had lost four of his prime years to the military, and this year he hadn't even been selected to represent the American League in the All Star game. But Feller knew he could still pitch. Maybe the fastball had lost some of its feared speed, but Feller was more than just a one-pitch pitcher. Among other things, his curveball was still the best in baseball. Physicists may call the curveball an 'optical illusion,' but don't tell that to the hitters who had to bat against Feller.

In fact, in a most unusual picture story, *Life* magazine and Feller proved that the thrown baseball *could* curve. Feller and *Life* set up tall poles at home plate, where a batter would stand, and a pole in back of home plate, where the catcher would crouch. With a high-speed camera, *Life* photographers took pictures of Feller's curveball. The pictures proved Feller – and the hitters – correct: He could indeed throw a ball so that it bent around poles.

In the game against Detroit, Mel Harder, the Indians' pitching coach, came to the mound as the fourth inning began and asked Feller how he felt. 'You don't look too good,' Harder commented. (This was after Feller had retired the first nine batters he had faced!) Feller assured him he was fine and continued to pitch. But Harder must have upset Feller's and his teammates' concentration, because two errors brought in a run for Detroit in the fourth inning, tying the game.

In the eighth the Indians came up with another run and gave Bobby the lead. His two previous no-hitters had

Bob Feller of the Indians pitches to Yankee Joe DiMaggio – 1946.

ABOVE: *George Kell, the Hall of Fame third baseman of the Detroit Tigers.*
RIGHT: *Slugging outfielder Vic Wertz of the Detroit Tigers.*

both been 1-0 games, so Feller was used to not having much run support when he pitched no-hitters. At the top of the ninth, Feller faced the heart of the Tiger line-up. Charlie Keller, the old Yankee star, was now a Detroit pinch hitter, and Feller got old King Kong Keller to fly out. Next was George Kell, another of the league's premier hitters, and Feller got Kell to bounce to short. Now it was Vic Wertz, the Tigers' leading home run slugger. Wertz ran the count to three and two, and Bobby Feller knew he was one strike away from accomplishing something no one has ever done. He fired his high, hard one, and Wertz swung – and missed.

It was Casey Stengel, as manager of the American League All Stars, who had decided not to select Feller for the All Star team. When he heard about the no-hitter, Stengel said, 'That cooks me. How could I know this guy was gonna pitch a no-hitter?' But with a pitcher like Bob Feller, a no-hitter was always more than just a possibility.

REYNOLDS'S SECOND NO-HITTER

They called him the Chief, and rightly so, because Allie Reynolds was one quarter Cheyenne Indian. By 1951 he had become the bell ringer of the Yankees' pitching staff. Earlier in the season Allie Reynolds out-pitched Bob Feller for his first no-hitter, winning 1-0. Now, in a doubleheader against the Boston Red Sox, the Yankees needed one win to clinch their third American League flag in a row.

In the first game it was Reynolds against Mel Parnell, the top Red Sox pitcher. The Red Sox were still one of the best-hitting teams in baseball, led by the matchless Ted Williams. Lou Boudreau had joined the Sox as playing manager, and his excellent hitting just made the Sox that much tougher. But the Red Sox had to sweep this doubleheader to stay in contention.

Reynolds set down the Red Sox in order in the top of the first, and his teammates got him two runs in their half of the first. Inning after inning Reynolds mowed down the Bosox, and with the exception of four walked batters, Reynolds was cruising. After six innings the Yankees led 5-0. Now the fans were warming to the drama in front of them. Everyone could see the zero under 'Hits' on the scoreboard, but in keeping with baseball tradition, no one said anything about a no-hitter for fear of jinxing Reynolds. In the Yankees dugout, none of the other players looked at him.

Three more Yankees scored, and as the first of the ninth opened, the Yankees led eight to nothing. Their pennant seemed certain, but now the focus of the drama had shifted. Facing

ABOVE: *Allie Reynolds, the ace of the Yankee pitching staff, won 182 games in his 13 years of play.*
BELOW: *Reynolds on the mound in 1951 – he was 17=8 that year.*

ABOVE: *Reynolds's very last pitch in his second no-hit, no-run game in 1951.*
LEFT: *Yankee catcher Yogi Berra grabs Ted Williams's pop fly for the final out.*

Reynolds was the heart of the Red Sox order, Dom DiMaggio, Johnny Pesky and Ted Williams. Reynolds got Dom to fly out to brother Joe in center field. Next Pesky bounced to Rizzuto, and he threw to Collins for out number two. Now baseball's greatest hitter stepped up. Reynolds threw two balls to Williams before he swung for a high pop-up behind the plate. Yogi Berra, one of the best catchers in the business, settled under the ball. Cheers turned to groans as the dependable Berra dropped the foul ball.

Reynolds patted Berra on the back. 'Don't worry Yogi, we'll get him again.' He was right.

Williams fouled off the next pitch, and Berra gave chase as the ball twisted towards the Yankees dugout. At the last moment Berra centered under the falling ball and caught it right in front of the dugout. The Yankees and Reynolds jumped on Yogi, celebrating their third pennant and, perhaps even more, the Chief's second no-hitter in one season, for that was a feat no pitcher in the American League had – or has – ever accomplished.

THOMSON'S THREE-RUN HOMER

Without question, the single most dramatic moment in baseball history took place at the Polo Grounds on 4 October 1951. In one of the most improbable scenarios in sports history, the New York Giants, 13½ games behind the Dodgers in mid-August, had come from behind to tie the Dodgers in the regular season. Starting on 12 August, Leo Durocher's Giants had won 39 games and had lost only eight. Now this astonishing race would have to be decided in a playoff.

The three-game playoff began in Brooklyn, where the Giants took a one-game lead. In the second game, played in the Polo Grounds, Brooklyn won 10-0. For the third and final game of the playoffs both teams went with their best pitchers: Sal 'The Barber' Maglie for the Giants and Don Newcombe for the Dodgers.

The Dodgers struck first when Maglie, who seldom gave up walks, after one out walked Pee Wee Reese and Duke Snider. Jackie Robinson followed with a single to left, and Reese came in to give the Dodgers the lead. In the second inning the Giants' Whitey Lockman singled, and Bobby Thomson next drove a hard smash to the leftfield corner. Thomson rounded first and, with his head down, raced towards second. But Lockman, waiting to see if Thomson's ball would be caught, only

RIGHT: *Giant Sal Maglie delivers a pitch in the 1951 playoff game.*
BELOW: *Pee Wee Reese is bowled over by the sliding Wes Westrum, who was forced out at second base.*

went as far as second. Thomson was run down by the Dodgers, the Giants didn't score and the rally ended.

After that, the Giants didn't threaten until the seventh, when Monte Irvin opened with a double. Lockman sacrificed, and Irvin reached third. Thomson's long fly ball to Duke Snider in center field scored Irvin, and the score was tied. But in the eighth, the Bums got to Maglie. Reese singled and moved to third on Snider's single. Maglie wild pitched, and Reese scored. After a walk to Jackie Robinson, Andy Pafco scratched a hit off Thomson's glove, and Snider scored. Billy Cox lined a hard single past Thomson at third, and Robinson scored. Three runs were in, and the Dodgers led 4-1. Maglie finally got the side out, but in the Giants' half of the eighth, Newcombe set them down in order.

Larry Jansen comes in to pitch for the Giants, and now he sets down the Dodgers in order in the top of the ninth. But the Dodgers don't seem to care. They know their pennant is just three outs away, and the Giants haven't had so much as a loud foul off Big Newk. The Dodgers can hear their fans chanting 'three more outs, three more outs' as they take the field for the

last of the ninth. Diehard Giants fans can take some consolation in the magnificent stretch run the team has made, but it looks as though that stretch run has taken all they had left.

The fans may be ready to quit, but the Giants aren't. They have been coming back all season, and they know they still have three outs to go. To quote a famous philosopher/catcher wearing Yankee pinstripes, 'It ain't over 'til its over.'

Alvin Dark, the Giants' captain and shortstop opens the ninth with a hard hit down first and off Gil Hodges' glove. Don Mueller slams a single to right, and the Giants faithful begin stirring. When Monte Irvin pops up, some of the air goes out of their sails, but then Whitey Lockman doubles to right, and Dark scores, to make the game 4-2. Mueller, running to third, slides and is safe but injures his left ankle and is carried from the field on a stretcher. Clint Hartung runs for him.

Now Charlie Dressen, manager of the Dodgers, takes out Don Newcombe. Big Newk has pitched the Dodgers into the playoffs, and he has had eight strong innings in this game. But Dressen thinks he's lost his stuff and brings in Ralph Branca. The Giants

ABOVE: Bobby Thomson hitting his playoff-winning home run against the Dodgers– 1951.

have runners on second and third, and first base is open. Dressen, catcher Rube Walker and Branca meet on the mound to discuss pitching to Thomson. With first base open, they can walk him and have a force-out at every base. Batting behind Thomson is Willie Mays, and the future Hall of Famer is having a dreadful playoff. They think they probably can get him out. But Dressen is a manager who believes that you don't put the winning run on base. So he tells Branca to pitch to Thomson.

Branca, a big, strong fastballer, warms up. Thomson, standing in the batters' circle, watches as Ralph fires one fastball after another into Walker's glove. Finally Branca signals he is ready, and the drama goes into high gear. Branca's first pitch is a strike. His second pitch is never called, because Thomson swings, and from the moment the ball leaves Thomson's bat there is no question that it is a home run!

ABOVE: *The entire Giant team, plus some fans, greet Thomson at home plate after his homer.*
RIGHT: *Manager Leo Durocher of the Giants with his playoff hero, Thomson.*

As Thomson rounds second on his way towards third, the stadium explodes. Giants players rush to home to greet Thomson. Eddie Stankey races around third and jumps on Leo Durocher in the coaching box at third. And Russ Hodges, the Giants' broadcaster, is screaming into his mike, 'The Giants win the pennant! The Giants' win the pennant! The Giants' win the pennant!' The roar from the stands cascades down on Thomson and his teammates, and thousands storm from the stands onto the field. When the Giants finally escape to their dressing room, the fans stand outside and chant for Thomson, and the smiling Scot makes a half dozen curtain calls. Inside, the champagne is flowing freely, and no one wants to shower.

Bobby Thomson's home run has been described as 'The Shot Heard 'Round The World.' To Ralph Branca and the Brooklyn Dodgers it was the incredible shot that killed their dreams for yet another year.

Mantle Hits the Longest Home Run

After the most thrilling chase in National League history, and still giddy from Thomson's memorable homer, the Giants were brought rudely back to earth by the Yankees in the 1951 World Series. Not only was this to be the Yankees' third straight Series victory, it also marked a significant change in the Yankee lineup. In Game Four the great Joe DiMaggio had hit a two-run homer, but it was to be his last as a Yankee. After the Series he retired. 'I'm not Joe DiMaggio any more,' he said sadly.

Of course everyone knew that this had to happen sometime, and none better than the Yankees' witty, gravelly-voiced manager, Charles Dillon 'Casey' Stengel. Ever since he had first come to the Yankees in 1949 Stengel had been busily platooning, trading and rebuilding the team with an eye towards ensuring that it would continue to be the powerhouse it had been since the days of Ruth. But by 1951, despite the Yankees' triumph in the Series, a large part of the sporting press was still far from convinced that

Stengel was succeeding. He was still new to the American League. His record as manager of the Braves and the Dodgers in the 30s and early 40s had been less than spectacular. And at the time when George Weiss, the Yankees' owner, had selected Stengel to manage the Bombers, Stengel had been reduced to managing the minor league team in his home town of Oakland, California.

Stengel had been grooming a young switch-hitter from Oklahoma named Mickey Mantle to take over DiMaggio's centerfield position when the Yankee Clipper stepped down. In the 1951 Series Mantle had underwhelmed everyone by getting only a bunt single in Game Two and then wrenching his knee and sitting out the rest of the Series. But Casey was not usually wrong about players' potential, and he certainly wasn't wrong about Mantle. By the end of the 1952 season it was clear that Mantle was a worthy successor to DiMaggio. In addition to

BELOW: *Joe DiMaggio (left) with future Yankee star and Hall of Famer Mickey Mantle.*

being a brilliant centerfielder, and despite the fact that, at 111, he led the American League in strikeouts, he was easily the Yankees' most dangerous hitter and probably, after Ted Williams, the most feared batter in the American League. And in the Yankees-Dodgers World Series that year Mantle fully justified his growing reputation, as the Yankees sailed to victory behind his inspired hitting.

Throughout his career Mantle contributed many great moments to baseball history, but to those who were lucky enough to witness it, none was more memorable than something he did on 18 April 1952 in a game against the Washington Senators at Griffith Stadium.

With two out in the fifth, and Yogi Berra on first, courtesy of a Chuck Stobbs walk, Mantle came to bat. It was early in the season, and Mantle had yet to hit his first home run of the year. Batting right-handed, Mantle blasted Stobbs's pitch over the leftfield fence at the 391-ft mark. As the ball cleared the fence and continued to climb, most thought it would bounce off the 55-foot fence in back of the wall. But it continued to soar, hitting the tip of the corner of the football scoreboard, bouncing out of the park and coming to rest in the back yard of a home across the street from the ball park. There is no telling how far the ball might have gone had it not nicked that scoreboard.

Many members of the press corps who had been following the Yankees since the days of Ruth and Gehrig insist that this was the most awesome clout they ever witnessed. Certainly the ball had gone where no ball had ever gone, and but for the scoreboard, the veteran pressmen insist, it would have been the longest home run in history. If so, it would have broken a record set by himself.

Mantle, in an exhibition game in Pittsburgh, cleared the rightfield roof. Before Mantle had rounded second, Arthur Patterson, a member of the Yankees' front-office staff, was seen running down the grandstand steps and heading out of the park. Patterson found a 10-year-old boy walking towards the stadium, carrying a baseball. Patterson grabbed the boy and asked where he had picked up the ball. The boy, Donald Dunaway, pointed to the spot. Patterson stepped off the distance and took the boy with him back to the game. After the game, young Dunaway gave the ball to Mantle, and Mickey gave him a replacement ball from the Yankees' locker room.

Patterson, doing some quick mathematics, figured out that Mantle had hit the ball about 565 feet. Interestingly, after that towering home run, Mantle

came up again and tried to drag a bunt to get on base. The bunt landed near second base and Mantle beat it out. Thus in one game, Mickey Mantle hit the longest home run on record and quite possibly the longest drag bunt in history.

ABOVE: *Billy Martin (left) with Mickey Mantle, who is holding the long-lost ball that he homered with.*
TOP: *Mantle hitting his home run in Griffith Stadium in Washington DC.*

THE YANKEES' FIFTH SERIES VICTORY

When Casey Stengel was named manager of the New York Yankees in 1949, he had some 40 years of baseball experience behind him as a player, coach and manager. But since none of those years had been spent in the American League and none of them had seemed particularly impressive, the New York press in 1949 openly questioned Stengel's credentials to manage the Yankees.

Four years and four World Championships later the press had come around and had dubbed Stengel 'The Ol' Perfesser.' Under him the Yankees had tied the record for consecutive World Series victories. Now, in 1953, as the Yankees headed into another Series with the Dodgers, the question was whether Stengel and his team were good enough to set a new record.

The team the Yankees had to beat had five .300 hitters: the National League's leading hitter, Carl Furillo; Roy Campenella, the RBI champion; Pee Wee Reese; Gil Hodges; and the irrepressible Jackie Robinson. The excellent Dodgers pitching staff was led by Carl Erskine, Preacher Roe, Johnny Podres and Joe Black. Of course the Yankees had the likes of Mickey Mantle, Yogi Berra and Hank Bauer, but in the Series to come the Yankee hero would be none of these. Rather, it would be a skinny second baseman whom Stengel had managed in the

BELOW: *Charles Dillon 'The Ol' Perfesser' Stengel, the manager of the New York Yankees.*

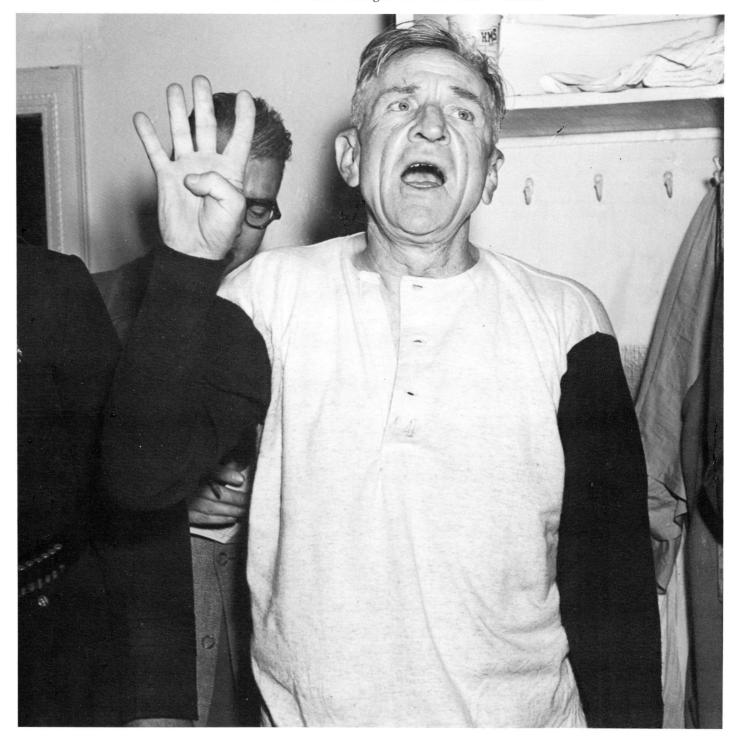

minors in Oakland, a player named Billy Martin.

In Game One, Martin tripled with the bases loaded in the first inning, and the Yankees rolled over the Dodgers 9-5. The winning pitcher was Johnny Sain, another of those National Leaguers Stengel kept picking up.

The Yankees won Game Two behind Eddie Lopat 4-2 and took their two-game-to-none lead to Ebbets Field for Game Three. There, Carl Erskine struck out 14 Yankees, a Series record, and the Dodgers won 3-2. They evened the Series in Game Four, beating Whitey Ford 7-3. In Game Five the Yankees scored five times in the third, routing Podres, and went on to an 11-7 win.

Back at Yankee Stadium, it was Ford against Erskine, but now Erskine failed to repeat his performance of Game Three, and the Yankees got two runs in the first. They added one in the second, and in the sixth Jackie Robinson decided that it was time for the Dodgers to do something. He doubled, stole third and scored on an infield out. But Ford got the side out and still took a 3-1 lead into the seventh. Then Stengel, in a surprise move, brought in Allie Reynolds from the bullpen after Ford gave up a single to Robinson.

Still leading 3-1, Reynolds got Gil Hodges to bounce out to open the ninth. He then walked Duke Snider and prepared to face Carl Furillo. The National League's leading hitter had had a good series, hitting over .300. Furillo brought the count to three and two and then smashed Reynolds's next pitch into the leftfield stands. As Snider scored and Furillo rounded the bases, Dodgers fans littered Yankee Stadium with confetti. The angry Reynolds struck out the next two Dodgers, but the damage had been done, and the Yankees went into their half of the ninth tied.

Clem Labine is now pitching for the Dodgers, and he walks Hank Bauer for openers. Yogi Berra flies out, and now Mickey Mantle is the batter. He tops a Labine pitch down third past Billy Cox for a single, and Bauer goes to second. Up steps Billy Martin, now the hitting star of the Series. The little second baseman has 11 hits in the Series, and his overall play has more than justified Stengel's faith in him.

Labine works carefully and has a count of one strike and a ball when Martin whacks Labine's third pitch over second, scoring Hank Bauer. So the Yankees win 4-3 and take the Series, four games to two. Thus the Brooklyn Dodgers fail for the seventh time in a World Series and must again wait 'til next year.

Billy Martin hit .500 in the series and was named the Most Valuable Player by the press. Casey Stengel, in just five seasons in the American League, had won an all-time record of five World Series banners. The Ol' Perfesser had shown the doubters once and for all. Now people were beginning to wonder if he wasn't the greatest manager in the history of the game.

The winning play of the 1953 World Series. TOP TO BOTTOM: *Billy Martin hits his game-winning single; Hank Bauer rounds third on his way to the plate; Bauer about to cross the plate with the winning run. Martin, the hero, had to be escorted to the dressing room by his teammates and the police to protect him from jubilant New York fans.*

MUSIAL'S FIVE HOME RUNS IN A DOUBLEHEADER

For years most people had considered Rogers Hornsby the greatest hitter in the history of the National League. Hornsby's stats certainly reflect what a great hitter he was, but since the early 1940s a graceful, lithe left-handed hitter from Donora, Pennsylvania, had had the experts reconsidering. By 1954 Stan Musial had already won six batting titles, and in 1948 Musial had a season that may have been the best individual season any hitter ever had.

BELOW: *Stanley Frank 'Stan the Man' Musial hitting his 1071st extra-base hit.*

ABOVE: *Musial played for the St Louis Cardinals for 22 years, hitting .331.*

The Cardinals' outfielder/first baseman led the National League in batting (.376), hits (230), slugging percentage (.702), runs scored (135), total bases (429), doubles (46), triples (18) and runs batted in (131). He also hit 39 home runs, and, had he hit one more, he'd have tied Johnny Mize and Ralph Kiner for the home run title. No hitter in history has ever led his league in every batting category, and only Stan Musial ever came so close.

Musial never thought of himself as a home run hitter, but no one would have demurred if he had. In fact, in one unforgettable doubleheader against the New York Giants, played on 3 May 1954, Stan the Man set a home run record. In the first game he walked on his first time up. But then, in the third and fifth innings, he hit two home runs. In the sixth he singled, and in the

eighth he smashed his third homer with two men on. As if this weren't impressive enough, in the second game, of his three hits two more were homers! In all, he had been at bat only eight times, yet he had hit five home runs and had driven in a total of nine runs. That his five homers in one doubleheader had set a record was almost of secondary importance to the fans who were privileged to witness this breathtaking demonstration of athletic ability.

When Musial had first come up to the big leagues veterans who saw his batting stance said he'd never make it. He would step into the batters' box, plant his left foot on the back line of the box, swing the bat over his head while wiggling his hips in kind of a hula movement, lightly put his right foot about 12 inches in front of his left foot and crouch. He held his arms away from his body with the bat pointed straight up. Teddy Lyons, the old White Sox pitcher who first saw Musial in the minors, described his stance to a

writer one day. 'Musial,' Lyons said, 'looks like a kid peeking around a corner to see if the cops are coming.' Musial never altered his stance in all the years he played, and it never failed to serve him well.

Henry Aaron called Stan Musial the greatest hitter he ever saw, and Ted Williams concurred, saying Stan Musial was the only hitter he ever saw who didn't shorten his grip when he had two strikes on him. Of all the many accolades Stan Musial received throughout his great career, the most moving was given in St Louis when Musial was presented a plaque. It read:

TO STANLEY FRANK MUSIAL, AN EMBLEM OF ESTEEM FROM HIS TEAM-MATES. AN OUTSTANDING ARTIST IN HIS PROFESSION; A GENTLEMAN IN EVERY SENSE OF THE WORD; ADORED AND WORSHIPED BY COUNTLESS THOU-SANDS; THE PERFECT ANSWER TO A MANAGER'S PRAYER; TO THIS WE (THE CARDINALS) ATTEST WITH OUR SIGNATURES.

THE GIANTS SWEEP THE 1954 SERIES

The New York Yankees did *not* win their sixth straight American League title in 1954: The honor of breaking the New York stranglehold on first place went to the Cleveland Indians. The Indians had the distinction of winning the most games in a single season in American League history, 111 games, well ahead of the Yankees, who won 103 games and finished second. The Cleveland team had great pitching, led by Bob Lemon and Early Wynn, who each won 23 games, followed by Mike Garcia, who won 19, and by Bob Feller, who won 13. This would be Feller's last winning season, and he would retire in a few more years. The Indians also had fair hitting, with Larry Doby supplying most of the home run power and Bobby Avila leading the league with an

ABOVE: *Bob Lemon, the ace right-hander for the Cleveland Indians.*
LEFT: *Manager Leo 'The Lip' Durocher of the New York Giants.*

average of .341. And finally, the Indians' defensive work, especially in the outfield, was excellent.

The Giants, on the other hand, had pretty much the same club that had lost to the Yankees in 1951, except that now Willie Mays was beginning to fulfil the promise of his natural talent. Their leading pitcher was Johnny Antonelli, who had won a respectable 21 games, but because the Cleveland pitching looked so formidable and because the Giants, with the exception of Mays, didn't look that awesome, the experts made Cleveland a heavy favorite.

Game One of this Series was easily one of the best World Series games ever played. The pitchers were Bob Lemon and Sal Maglie. In the first inning the hitting star for the Indians, Vic Wertz, hit a triple to score two runs for the Indians. The Giants tied the score in the third, and then the two pitchers settled down to throw shutout innings at each other. But in the eighth, Sal Maglie began to falter. First he gave

Giant outfielder Willie Mays about to catch a Vic Wertz-hit ball (above). After making the catch over his shoulder, Mays (left) whirls to peg the ball into the infield.

up a walk to Larry Doby, and then, when Al Rosen singled up the middle, Leo Durocher went to his bullpen and brought in lefthander Don Liddle. The first man he had to face was Vic Wertz, who already had three of the Indians' hits and had driven in their two runs.

What happened next is today considered the greatest fielding play in World Series history. The powerful Wertz smashed a Liddle pitch to the deepest part of the Polo Grounds, 505 ft away. As the ball left Wertz's bat, Willie Mays turned and ran as hard as he could towards the wall. Looking behind him as he sped towards the fence, Mays reached up with his gloved left hand and caught the ball over his right shoulder. Then Mays stopped, somehow wheeled and threw the ball to the infield, almost doubling off the Indians runners who thought the ball would never be caught.

In the tenth inning, Mays, who had gone hitless in the game, led off with a walk. Lemon was still pitching, and while he was being over-cautious with hitter Henry Thompson, Willie Mays stole second. That instantly changed the strategy of the Indians' Manager, Al Lopez. He ordered Lemon to walk Thompson and to pitch to Monte Irvin. But Durocher countered with his pinch-hitter, Dusty Rhodes.

The big South Carolinan made Leo the Lip look like a genius when he pulled Lemon's first pitch down the rightfield line. The high pop-up traveled to the shortest part of the Polo Grounds, the rightfield wall, 297 ft away. The ball came down and bounced on the top of the wall for a home run! The Giants win 5-2.

The rest of the series was anticlimactic. Everyone was talking about Mays's catch of Wertz's drive and about Rhodes's homer. The two plays seemed to have taken the heart out of the Indians. They dropped the next three straight as the Giants completed the sweep of the league champions.

ABOVE: *Fans chase their Giants into the clubhouse after the game as the Pirates leave at left.*
RIGHT: *James LaMar 'Dusty' Rhodes, the Giants' pinch-hitting hero.*

For some reason, even though he had a 13-3 record, Bob Feller didn't pitch in the Series. Lopez sent in Bob Lemon for the fourth game, even though he was deluged by calls from Cleveland fans to give Feller a start. Feller would never appear in another World Series game, and neither would the Cleveland Indians. For that matter, there would never be another Series played in the Polo Grounds. Although no one fully understood it at the time, baseball was undergoing a fundamental change. The move by the Braves to Milwaukee and the Browns to Baltimore was only the beginning. Soon, the venerable Connie Mack would sell his Philadelphia Athletics, and the new owners would move to the heartland of the United States, Kansas City, Missouri.

THE DODGERS WIN THEIR FIRST SERIES

The Brooklyn Dodgers had played in seven World Series and never won one. In the early days of the game, in 1916 and 1920, they lost to Boston and Cleveland. Between 1941 and 1955 the Dodgers had appeared in five Series and lost them all to the New York Yankees. If many baseball fans thought that the World Series seemed always to be between the Yankees and the Dodgers, they were partly correct. Starting with 1941, when Mickey Owen's passed ball cost them the Series, the Dodgers had played in 35 percent of the Series played between then and 1955. The New York Yankees had played in 75 percent of them.

Now, in 1955, the Dodgers came into the Series with a team that had run away with the National League pennant, winning 22 of their first 24 games after the season opened. They had five players who hit over .300, the League's Most Valuable Player in Roy Campanella and its leading hitter in Carl Furillo. Don Newcombe won 20 games,

and such players as Reese, Snider, Hodges and Jackie Robinson made the Dodgers feared opponents. Yet still they would be playing the New York Yankees, the team that somehow always beat the Dodgers.

No fans suffered like Dodgers fans. For years the team was the laughing-stock of the National League, but when Larry MacPhail and Branch Rickey took over, the Dodgers became winners. Along with the St Louis Cardinals, the Dodgers were the power in the National League from the beginning of World War II until very recently. But no matter what the Dodgers did, the hated, haughty New York Yankees seemed always ready to spoil their World Series.

After missing a World Series appearance in 1954, the Yankees resumed their accustomed place in the American League, ie on top. Mickey Mantle had proven a more than worthy successor to Joe DiMaggio, and with Yogi Berra, Phil Rizzuto, Bill Skowron, Hank Bauer and Whitey Ford leading the pitching, this 1955 Yankee team was as good as any of the ones that had won five World Series in a row.

Casey Stengel was again managing in a World Series, his sixth in seven years at the helm of the Yankees. His managerial opponent was Walter Alston, now in his second year with the Dodgers and a troubled man because three of his stars, Jackie Robinson, Roy Campenella and Don Newcombe, had publicly disagreed with some of his decisions. Alston forced all three to back down, but the strain be-

tween the manager and the players was fodder for the always bloodthirsty New York press, which definitely did not put Walter Alston in a class with Casey Stengel. If the Series were to be decided by the ability of the manager, Stengel would be the easy winner, according to the experts.

Misfortune in the form of injuries

BOTTOM: *Ace batter Mickey Mantle, manager Casey Stengel and ace pitcher Whitey Ford of the Yankees.*
BELOW: *Carl Anthony 'Skoonj,' Furillo of the Brooklyn/Los Angeles Dodgers.*

LEFT: *Yankee Billy Martin is called out at home after an attempted steal.*
BOTTOM: *Yankee Bill Skowron kicks the ball out of the hand of Dodger catcher Roy Campanella.*

hurt both teams. Jackie Robinson could only play in the first three games, after which the injury to his Achilles tendon proved too painful. Mickey Mantle had knee injuries and would miss most of the Series. But both teams were rich in talented players to fill in.

Whitey Ford won the first game for the Yankees 6-5 as first baseman Joe Collins hit two home runs off Don Newcombe. In Game Two Stengel went with another lefthander, Tommy Byrne, and it worked, as the Yankees took a two-game lead.

Crossing the East River from the Bronx to Brooklyn, the teams met at Ebbets Field, and young lefthander Johnny Podres was Alston's selection to stop the Yankees. He did, on a five-hitter, and celebrated his 23rd birthday with his first World Series victory. Roy Campanella's two-run homer gave Podres the lead, and the Dodgers went on to win 8-3. In Game Four it was the Dodgers again, as they bombed the Yankees 8-5, beating Don Larsen and four other Yankees pitchers. In Game Five the Dodgers hit three thunderous home runs (Duke Snider getting two) as the Dodgers' young Roger Craig held the Yankees in check to win his first World Series game 5-3.

The redoubtable Whitey Ford pulled the Yankees even when the Series came back to the Bronx, holding the Dodgers to four hits and winning 5-1. Now the Series was tied. The seventh and final game would pit Tommy Byrne of the Yankees, winner of Game Two, against Johnny Podres, winner of Game Three. Because Jackie Robinson was injured, Don Hoak would play his position at third base, Junior Gilliam would play left field instead of second, his normal position and Don Zimmer would play second for the Dodgers.

For three innings, Podres and Byrne close the doors, but in the fourth, Campanella doubles to right and comes home on a Gil Hodges single. In the sixth, Reese opens with a hit, and Duke Snider sacrifices. Byrne picks up the ball and flips to Bill Skowron at first. But Skowron doesn't touch the bag and tries to tag Snider out. Snider's elbow knocks the ball out of Skowron's glove, and suddenly the Dodgers have two men on, no outs.

Campanella sacrifices and Snider and Reese advance. Stengel tells Byrne to walk Carl Furillo, and the Dodgers load the bases. Stengel brings in Bob Grim, but Gil Hodges hits a long fly deep to center, and Reese scores from

RIGHT: *The Dodgers' star left-hander, Johnny Podres, pitching in the seventh Series game, 1955.*
BOTTOM RIGHT: *Dodger left fielder Sandy Amoros catching Yogi Berra's fly ball.*

third after the catch. Dodgers 2, Yankees 0.

Grim walks Hoak and fills the bases again. Alston brings in a pinch-hitter for Zimmer, and the hitter, George Shuba, grounds out to end the inning. But Alston is not too disappointed, for all this is part of a plan. With Zimmer out for a pinch-hitter, Alston now moves Junior Gilliam in from left field to his normal position, second base, and puts the speedy, sure-handed Sandy Amoros into left field.

Billy Martin coaxes a walk out of Podres as the Yankees lead off their half of the sixth. Gil McDougald attempts to sacrifice for Martin and beats out his bunt. With Yankees on first and second, the ever-dangerous Yogi Berra comes to bat. A notorious bad-ball hitter and one of the great clutch hitters in the game, Berra is the Yankees' most feared batter. He strokes a drive towards the corner in left field, and the hit has double written all over it. Martin starts towards third but keeps watching the Dodgers' Amoros chase Berra's fly ball. McDougald, assuming a double, heads for second with his head down. Amoros, running all out catches up with Berra's ball and grabs it just before it hits the ground in fair territory. Amoros hits the wall but holds on to the ball, whirls and throws to his cut-off man, Reese. Reese sees Martin going back to second and McDougald desperately trying to get back to first. A strong throw to Hodges, and McDougald is doubled up by inches, and the Yankees are in deep trouble.

In the eighth the Yankees make their final run at Podres. Rizzuto singles, but Martin flies out. McDougald smashes a ball down third, and when it bounces off Hoak's shoulder they have two on with one out. Coming up for the Yankees are Berra and Bauer. Podres now reaches down and becomes the Pride of Flatbush. He gets Berra on a fly to right and then strikes out Bauer to the cheers of all the Dodgers fans in the stadium and the millions watching on television. It is all over. Nothing happens in the ninth, and when the last Yankee is out, Podres is mobbed by his teammates, and Brooklyn goes wild. The Bums have finally won the World Series, and Walter Alston has quietly put his stamp on the Dodgers and gained the respect of his peers and the press. Brooklyn finally is the capital of the world of baseball, and to make it even sweeter, the Bums beat the Yanks.

DON LARSEN'S PERFECT GAME

One of baseball's truly great moments occurred in Yankee Stadium on 8 October 1956. On that hazy fall afternoon Don Larsen moved into baseball's Hall of Fame by pitching a perfect World Series game, beating the Brooklyn Dodgers 2-0 to win Game Five and give the Yankees a three-games-to-two lead over the Dodgers.

That Larsen was even pitching for the Yankees was in itself a story. Even though he had all the physical assets to be a winning pitcher, his carefree, flamboyant personality had taken Don Larsen on an odyssey through the teams of the American League.

Training, conditioning and sleep were words that Larsen heard but paid no attention to. When Larsen came up to the majors with the dreadful St Louis Browns he won seven and lost 12. The next year, when the Browns became the Baltimore Orioles, his record was a dismal 3-21. Two of his three victories came against the Yankees, and in the wonderful way baseball has of getting the right man with the right team, those two victories impressed Casey Stengel, so when the Yankees engineered a mammoth 18-player trade, Larsen was one of the players Stengel wanted and got. But even after he came to the Yankees, Don Larsen went his own undisciplined way, and Stengel finally shipped him off to the team's Denver farm club, only to recall him late in 1955 and watch him lose Game Four of the Series.

During the season, the Yankees had been in Boston for a game with the Red Sox when Larsen was pitching. It had seemed to him that the Red Sox third base coach was stealing his pitches, so he had tried a new windup. Larsen, like most pitchers, had always planted his foot on the rubber, rocked back and forth and wound up so his hands would go above his head. As he strode forward to deliver the ball, his hand would leave his mitt as he moved into his pitch. Because he was tall, with his hand open above his head, Larsen's grip on the ball was visible, and after a while it was easy for a coach to flash a signal – fastball or curve – to the batter. The batter could pick up the sign even before Larsen had wound up.

So Larsen had decided not to bring

TOP RIGHT: *Yankee Manager Casey Stengel pats the head of pitcher Don Larsen after the perfect game.*
RIGHT: *Right-hander Larsen threw only 97 pitches in his perfect World Series victory.*

the ball above his head, but to use no windup and just bring his hands to his shoulder, stride and throw. It was called the no-windup, and once Larsen had perfected it, he began winning.

1956 had seen Mickey Mantle win the triple crown and lead the Yankees to another American League pennant. The Dodgers, on the other hand, the defending World Champions, had had to fight for their lives to make it back to the Series. A young, talented Milwaukee Braves team had led them most of the season, only to have the Dodgers win on the last day.

In mid-season the Dodgers had picked up an old paladin from the junk heap of baseball. At 39 years of age, Sal 'The Barber' Maglie, the once-magnificent New York Giants pitcher who had so tormented the Dodgers over the years, was declared a free agent. Nobody in baseball much wanted Maglie, but when the Cleveland Indians let him go early in the season, the Dodgers had picked him up. This had proved to be the making of their season and the main reason they had made it to the World Series.

In the opener at Ebbets Field, Sal Maglie was wonderful, outpitching Whitey Ford and beating the Yankees 6-3. The Dodgers next blasted the Yankees 13-8, and as they left Ebbets Field for Yankee Stadium, the Dodgers

ABOVE: *Enos 'Country' Slaughter after hitting his three-run homer for the Yankees in the Series.*

TOP RIGHT: *Salvatore 'Sal the Barber' Maglie, the Dodgers' pitcher.*

felt they had a chance of beating the Yankees for the second year in a row. But Ford and the Yankees came back and took Game Three 5-3 and then took Game Four 6-2. Now it was Sal Maglie again against Don Larsen in Game Five.

In Game Two, Larsen had been one of seven pitchers whom the Dodgers had battered. Now, with Maglie going for them and the inconsistent Larsen on the mound for the Pinstripers, the Dodgers thought they were in the catbird seat. The night before Larsen pitched in Game Two, Casey Stengel had told him to get a good night's sleep. He did and was shelled by the Bums. Knowing he was going to pitch Game Five, Larsen reverted to his own kind of regime and hoisted a few before getting to bed well after midnight. But when he went to the mound against the Dodgers that early fall afternoon he knew he had to be sharp because Maglie was bound to be.

In fact, both pitchers were at the top of their form. For three innings, backed up by superlative fielding, neither Maglie nor Larsen allowed the other side a run. Finally, in the fourth, Mickey Mantle homered into the right centerfield bleachers to give the Yankees a 1-0 lead. There seemed every

chance that the Dodgers would retaliate in the fifth, but Larsen continued to hold them scoreless.

As they went into the sixth, the huge crowd began to stir. Up till now, they had appreciated the fine pitchers' duel between Larsen, with his no-windup delivery, and the ancient competitor, Sal Maglie. But as Larsen walked to the mound for the start of the sixth, people seemed to sense that something else might be happening. They could see on the scoreboard that there hadn't been a Brooklyn hit, and from now on each pitch added to the gathering tension.

Furillo and Campanella go down on pop-ups to Billy Martin, and Larsen strikes out his counterpart, Sal Maglie. The Yankees get to Maglie in the bottom of the sixth for a second run. Now, as the tension increases, Larsen seems to be the calmest man in Yankee Stadium. Jim Gilliam hits a curve sharply to McDougald, who throws him out. The cheers are loud but short as everyone waits for the next batter and the next pitch. Reese flies to Mantle, and Snider flies to Slaughter in left as the top of the seventh ends. The Yankees' fans stand for the seventh inning stretch. By now most of them know what Larsen has going, but few

ABOVE: *Dale Mitchell, the Dodger outfielder who made the last out.*
RIGHT: *Yogi Berra hugs Larsen.*
BOTTOM RIGHT: *Larsen is mobbed.*

people in the crowd of 66,000 want to talk about it. Newspapermen can only look at each other and observe the time-honored tradition of not saying the jinx word 'no-hitter.'

Eighth inning. Jackie Robinson is up, and if anyone wanted to bet, more money would be placed on Robinson as the man who'd break up the no-hitter than on any Dodgers player. But Robinson only bounces back to Larsen, who throws him out. Down go Hodges and Amoros, and now the crowd stands and gives Larsen a standing ovation. The pitcher shuffles into the dugout as if he and Yogi had just been playing catch.

For eight innings, Don Larsen has held one of baseball's greatest hitting teams off the bases. but it will be the ninth that will decide whether this performance is something more than exceptional.

Furillo fouls off the first two pitches and then, in what seems an eternity,

fouls off two more before mercifully flying out to Hank Bauer in right field. Twenty-fifth man, 25th out. Campanella wrings a gasp from the crowd when he hits a high drive towards the leftfield stands, but the ball sails harmlessly into the stands, foul. A curve, Campy swings and the ball is a short pop-up to Martin.

Now Walter Alston sends in a pinch-hitter for Sal Maglie. The batter is Dale Mitchell, formerly a Cleveland Indian and a batter who seldom strikes out. First pitch, ball one, low, and the stadium groans. A slow curve, and Mitchell lays off it, but umpire Babe Pinelli's right hand goes up: strike one. Now Larsen is no longer a calm, nonchalant pitcher. He bears down with all he has and fires a good fastball that Mitchell swings at and misses. One

ball, two strikes. Another fastball, but Mitchell's quick bat gets to it and fouls it off. More groans, more twisting in seats, more prayers for Don Larsen.

Berra signals for another fastball, and Larsen begins his delivery. The ball comes in on the outside corner, knee high. Mitchell cocks but can't pull the trigger. Berra is up and running for Larsen as Umpire Pinelli pumps that right hand. Strike three!

Berra hurls himself into Larsen's arms as the Yankees rush out of the dugout and come in from the field to hug and whack their hero. Thousands pour on to the field to try and touch Larsen. Men who have covered baseball since Cy Young and Honus Wagner sit staring at their typewriters. Broadcasters are at a loss for words, finding perfection all but indescribable.

The Braves Win the 1957 Series

The 1957 Milwaukee Braves came into the Series against the Yankees with a powerful batting lineup, headed by Hank Aaron, slugging Eddie Mathews and Joe Adcock. Red Schoendienst, too, had come to the Braves after a brilliant career with St Louis, and his presence had settled down the Braves' infield, making it one of the best in the game. Warren Spahn headed a pitching staff that included Bob Buhl and Lew Burdette. In 1956 Burdette had led the National League in lowest ERA, but his 1957 season had been, so far, less impressive.

The Yankees were . . . well, the Yankees, and along with Mantle there were the familiar crew of Berra, Bauer, Skowron, McDougald and a versatile

ABOVE: *Pitcher Warren Spahn of the Milwaukee Braves throwing in the fourth World Series game in 1957.*
BELOW: *Yankee catcher Yogi Berra scores on a squeeze play in the 1957 World Series.*

ABOVE: *Jut-jawed Milwaukee pitching ace Lew Burdette in action in the World Series.*
RIGHT: *Frank Torre of the Braves is forced at second in the front end of a double play in the Series.*

rookie from Wisconsin, Tony Kubek. Whitey Ford was again the ace of the pitching staff, and Don Larsen was ready to try to repeat his historic performance in the last World Series.

In Game One, the fans saw a classic duel between the two finest left-handers of their day, Whitey Ford and Warren Spahn. In the end Ford bested Spahn 3-1. In Game Two it was Bob Turley for the Yankees and Lew Burdette for Milwaukee. Burdette was facing the team he originally signed with. Casey Stengel, during the pennant drive of 1951, had traded with the Boston Braves to get Johnny Sain. The Braves got $50,000 and a rookie pitcher in the Yankees' farm system, Lew Burdette. So Burdette had something to prove to Stengel, and he did, winning Game Two 4-2.

The Yankees came back to rout the Braves 12-3, with the local boy, Tony Kubek of the Yankees, leading the way with two home runs, much to the displeasure of the Milwaukee fans. Spahn won the next game 7-5, after blowing a 4-1 lead to the Yankees, who tied it in the ninth with three runs and went ahead in the tenth when Kubek singled and Bauer tripled. But Spahn and the Braves then got a lucky, if somewhat bizarre, break. Nippy Jones was pinch-hitting, and after one inside pitch, he spun away from the ball and trotted down to first. The umpire called him back. Jones said he had been hit by the pitch, but with the Yankees screaming, the umpire said he wasn't and ordered Jones to hit. Jones asked to see the ball, and when the umpire and the Yankees looked at it, there was the scuff mark made from the black shoe polish on Jones's right shoe. Down to first went Jones. Felix Mantilla was ordered to run for the 'shoe polish kid,' and Red Schoendienst promptly sacrificed Mantilla to second. Johnny Logan brought him home with a double to tie the game, and then Eddie Mathews won it with his first World Series home run.

Burdette pitched in the fifth game, and this time he faced the Yankees' ace, Whitey Ford. They fought a great duel, and Burdette threw a seven-hitter, winning it 1-0, thus giving the Braves a three-games-to-two lead in the Series. In the sixth game, in Yankee Stadium, the Yankees tied it all up again by winning 3-2.

Now it was the seventh and final game, and the Braves announced that Warren Spahn, their ace and scheduled pitcher, was out with influenza. Manager Fred Haney handed the ball to Lew Burdette, who would have to pitch with only two days rest. While not overpoweringly fast, Burdette had a good a slider, curve and screwball, plus excellent control. He also had something else going for him. Burdette, many claimed, threw a spitball, and through the Series the Yankees had tried their damnedest to get Burdette off stride by telling the umpire to look at the ball. Burdette always denied that he threw a spitter, but he liked to worry the hitters, so sometimes he made it look as if he were lifting the ball to his mouth. In any case, Burdette was such a mean, tough competitor that the sight of his menacing face peering in from the mound left many batters with the feeling that Burdette would have no compunction about throwing the ball at their heads.

Now with the Series riding on his right arm, the crafty Burdette could be

looking at immortality, for only the great Christy Mathewson had won three complete games in the World Series, and that was back in the days of the dead ball. On the other hand, Burdette was facing one of the best-hitting teams in the game, with a live ball and a short porch in right field. And his mound opponent was Don Larsen.

Burdette gets through the first inning thanks to bad base running by the Yankees. He sets them down in the next two innings, and in the top of the third, the Braves grab the lead when, after Burdette fouls out, rookie Bob Hazle singles to left and Logan slams a groundball to Kubek at third. This most steady and versatile of the Yankees makes a good play on the ball and throws to second to try to start a double play. But his throw pulls Jerry Coleman off second, and the runner is safe. Coleman throws to first to try to get Logan, but Logan just makes it. Eddie Mathews then brings them both home with a double down the right-field line, and Stengel takes out Larsen.

Henry Aaron greets Bobby Schanz, the Yankees' reliever, with a single to center that brings Mathews home. Wes Covington singles Aaron to third, and when the Yankees can't turn Frank

Torre's grounder into a double play, Aaron scores, and it is Braves – 4, Yankees – 0.

Now Burdette has an almost insurmountable lead, and he warms to his task. A base hit here and there, but the Yankees can't get a runner past first. Mixing his sliders, sinkers and curves with an occasional trip to his mouth for maximum effect, Burdette mows down the New Yorkers, shutting them out inning after inning.

Now comes the ninth inning, the Yankees' last chance. The shadows have lengthed in the huge park, and Burdette is tired. He has pitched 26 innings, given up only two runs and has shut out the Yankees for 23 innings. Can he make it 24, or will the potent Yankee bats come to life against their tormentor?

The Yankees attack. Berra pops up for the first out, but then McDougald singles. Tony Kubek drives the ball deep to right center, but Hank Aaron runs it down. Now the Yankees know Burdette is tired, but can they get to him? They try their best. Jerry Coleman singles. Tommy Byrne hits a hot smash towards the hole at second, but Felix Mantilla dives at the ball and knocks it down for a single. Trailing by five runs, the Yankees don't try to get McDou-

Braves shortstop Johnny Logan tags Yankee catcher Yogi Berra as he tried to get back to second base.

gald in and hold him at third, loading the bases. Now Burdette faces Moose Skowron, a powerful hitter who can get the Yankees to within one run with a single swing of the bat.

Burdette sucks in his gut and throws. Yankee fans are pleading for the Moose, and he obliges by hitting a hard grounder towards third. Eddie Mathews, the fielding star of the Series, make a great stop, steps on third for the force, the Milwaukee Braves are the World Champions and Lew Burdette has won three complete World Series games, shutting out the New York Yankees for 24 consecutive innings.

Back in March 1953, when the rumors had been strong that Milwaukee might get a major league team, over 15,000 Wisconsinites had massed at night in the freezing cold and snow of Country Stadium to await the announcement that the Braves were coming. Now, five seasons later, thanks to many players, and especially to Lew Burdette, the Beer Capital of the World was also baseball's capital.

HARVEY HADDIX'S PERFECT GAME

He broke into major league baseball with the St Louis Cardinals in 1952, and the next year he won 20 games for the Redbirds. His name was Harvey Haddix, and he was a slight, wiry left-hander. He reminded many Cardinals players of Harry 'The Cat' Brecheen, the hero of the 1946 World Series, so if Brecheen was 'The Cat,' Haddix would be called 'The Kitten.'

The nickname stuck, but Haddix didn't. The Cards traded him to the Phillies after three years, and they in turn traded him after a few seasons to the Pirates. To most baseball people, Harvey Haddix was a fine pitcher, but one who had never completely fulfilled his potential.

Yet on a humid, overcast night in Milwaukee on 27 May 1959 Harvey Haddix pitched what was in some ways the greatest game ever thrown and assured himself a place in the Hall of Fame. Against the best-hitting team playing in the National League, Harvey Haddix held the Braves hitless for 12 innings. Further, not one Brave reached first base. There were no errors, walks or passed balls. With his slider working to perfection, and his curve nicking the corners of home plate, Haddix saw 36 Braves come to bat and 36 sit down again.

Unfortunately for Haddix, his Pirate teammates couldn't get a run off Lew Burdette of the Braves. Inning after inning one or two Pirates would get on base and threaten, but Burdette always came up with a pitch to get out of the jam. And finally, in the bottom of the 13th, Harvey Haddix's dream came crashing down. A groundball to third baseman Don Hoak broke the spell. Hoak fielded it cleanly, but his throw to first bounced on the ground, and when the first baseman, Rockey Nelson, couldn't handle it, Felix Mantilla, the hitter, was on first, thanks to an error. One man had finally reached first. The perfect game was gone, but Haddix still had the no-hitter.

Eddie Mathews sacrificed Mantilla to second, bringing up Hank Aaron. The brilliant young centerfielder of the Braves was leading the league in hitting at that time, batting .442, and Haddix decided to walk such a dangerous hitter. Up stepped Joe Adcock, the powerful first baseman who, a few years earlier, had hit four home runs in a game. Haddix had earlier struck out Adcock twice, but this time Haddix's slider didn't fool Adcock, who hit a long drive to right center, clearing the fence. And so it was over. Haddix hadn't pitched a no-hitter and the Pirates had lost the game.

But it *had* been a perfect game for 12 entire innings, something unexampled in baseball before or since. And, on top of that, for it to have been a loss . . . ! The sportswriters simply couldn't believe they had seen what they had just seen.

Afterwards, Haddix told reporters that he had been tired and had just hung a slider. 'Can't do that to a hitter like Adcock,' said Haddix gloomily. The earnest question that ended the press conference came from a cub reporter. 'Harvey,' the young man asked, 'was that the best game you ever pitched?'

BELOW: *Pittsburgh Pirates pitcher Harvey Haddix delivers the ball.*

So Long Teddy Ballgame

As the 1960 season wore down to the end, the Yankees had locked up another American League title, the 10th in Casey Stengel's 12-year tenure as manager of the Bronx Bombers. Over in the National League, the Pittsburgh Pirates were threatening to win their first National League title since the days of high button shoes and Honus Wagner. And in Boston, an institution was about to retire.

In 1959 Ted Williams had hit only .254 in an injury-filled season, the only time he had hit below .300 in his 21-year career. Many felt that Ted should retire then, but he decided that he didn't want to end his career on a .250 season.

Going out in fashion, Williams hit .316 and 29 homers in just a little over 300 at bats. He had already told the Red Sox management that he would retire after the 1960 season. On the last day of the season the Bosox were hosting the Baltimore Orioles. When Williams came to bat in the bottom of the eighth, his last time, the Boston fans gave him a standing ovation. Williams had never tipped his hat to acknowledge fan applause in his whole career with Boston, and he didn't do so now.

As he stepped into the box to face young Jack Fisher, he was determined that this would be his last time at bat. He had no intention of seeing the Orioles tie the score and have the game go into extra innings. Fisher threw a ball and then a pitch right down the middle. Williams swung and missed. He was stunned. Never in his life had he missed a pitch like that. When he looked out at Fisher on the mound, the youngster was smiling and signaling his catcher to throw the ball back.

Fisher couldn't wait to throw another strike past the once-formidable hitter who now stood facing him in the batters' box.

Williams steps in and waits. Fisher throws, and it is the same pitch. Ted swings, and the ball leaps off his bat, climbing high in the sky towards the rightfield bleachers. As the Boston fans stand and roar, Williams lopes around the bases with his head down, in that strange trot of his, where his left shoulder leans forward, like he's running against a gale. Around third, past home and, still running, into the dugout, shaking hands with the rest of the Sox, into the club house and the Hall of Fame. And not once had his hand touched his cap.

BELOW: *Outfielder Ted Williams gets his last hit as a member of the Boston Red Sox.*

Bill Mazeroski's Homer

The last time the Pittsburgh Pirates played in a World Series, Calvin Coolidge was President and Prohibition was making millionaires out of bootleggers. For 35 years, the fans of the Steel City's team had suffered one dismal season after another. Their greatest hero was still Honus Wagner, a player who had stopped playing before most Pirates fans were born.

None of the 1960 Pirates had been present to experience the embarrassment that the 1927 Pirates had suffered at the hands of the Yankees' Murderers' Row when Ruth and company swept the Pirates in the Series, but most of them could remember that only a few years ago the Pirates had lost the most games in a season in the history of baseball. But now they had some talent, especially a young Puerto Rican named Roberto Clemente and two fine infielders, Dick Groat and Bill Mazeroski. And their pitching was good, led by Vernon Law and a great relief pitcher, Elroy Face. But of course the odds-makers heavily favored Mantle, Berra, Skowron, Kubek, Howard and the new Yankee, Roger Maris.

The Series had nevertheless come down to a seventh game at ancient Forbes Field in Pittsburgh. In Game

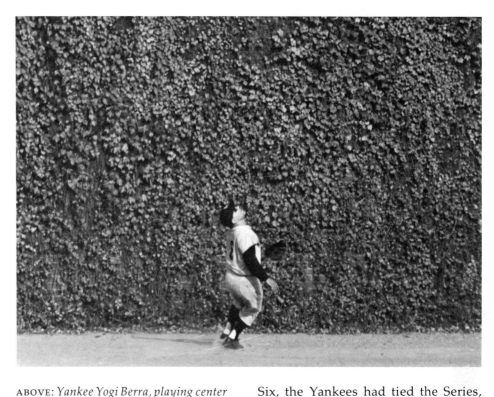

ABOVE: *Yankee Yogi Berra, playing center field for a change, watches Mazeroski's home run go over the wall of Pittsburgh's Forbes Field.*
BELOW: *Yankee pitcher Whitey Ford singles in the second inning of the sixth World Series game in 1960 in Pittsburgh.*

Six, the Yankees had tied the Series, blasting the Pirates 12-0. Now the Bucs jumped off to a four-run lead, scoring twice in each of the first two innings. The Yankees got a Skowron homer in the fifth and then, in the sixth, scored four more, knocking out Vernon Law and taking a 5-4 lead. The Yankees added two more in their half of the eighth and were leading 7-4 when all hell broke loose.

The Pirates' Gino Cimoli pinch-hits a single, and Dick Groat then hits a hard bouncer to Tony Kubek at short. As Kubek bends down to pick up the grounder, the ball strikes a stone on the infield and bounces up, smashing Kubek in the throat and knocking him to the ground in terrible pain. After they rush Kubek to the hospital for observation, the next two hitters are put out. But Clemente gets a running single, scoring Cimoli, and the next batter, Hal Smith, a former Yankee farm hand, smacks a three-run homer, giving the Pirates a 9-7 lead going into the ninth.

The Yankees come back to tie in their half of the ninth. Now the Pirates come to bat. If they can make just one run they will win the Series. If they don't, they could lose it. Mazeroski faces Ralph Terry and takes the first pitch for a ball. Terry's next pitch is a fastball, and when Mazeroski hits it, Forbes Field shakes to its very foundations, for it is unquestionably a home run. The jubilant Mazeroski is jumping up and

ABOVE: *Bill Mazeroski is met by excited fans as he rounds the bases after his homer.*

down as he rounds the bases, and he almost is knocked over by Pirates fans as he tries to touch home plate, where the Pirates wait to maul him.

Bill Mazeroski, who grew up in the shadows of the steel mills of Pitts-

burgh, was probably the most appropriate man imaginable to have scored the run that, after 35 empty years, at last returned the World Championship to the Pirates.

But in so doing he may have contributed to the downfall of a great man. A few weeks later, the Yankees announced that Casey Stengel had been fired. Stating that Stengel has reached

70, the Yankees replaced The Ol' Perfesser with Ralph Houk, a third-string catcher and now a coach under Stengel. Stengel, who had brought the Yankees 10 American League pennants and seven World Championships in his 12 years, could not disguise his bitterness when he appeared before the press. 'I'll never make the mistake of being 70 again,' he said.

ROGER MARIS'S 61ST HOME RUN

By 1961 the American League had expanded to 10 teams. The Angels had been established in Los Angeles, the original Senators had moved to Minneapolis/St Paul and a new Senators team had been created in Washington. Because of this expansion the league owners decided to increase the number of seasonal games played to determine the pennant winner from 154 to 162. Little did anyone guess what controversy this apparently simple and logical decision would soon cause.

The Yankees were still the powerhouse of the American League, and as the '61 season opened they had a new star to add to their pantheon. In 1960 they had acquired a young player named Roger Maris from the Kansas City Athletics, and in that year Maris had hit no less than 39 home runs – only one less than Mickey Mantle – and had, in addition, proven to be such an excellent fielder that he was named the league's MVP.

Maris was a superb all-round athlete. While still in high school in Fargo, North Dakota, he had been offered several football scholarships, but he had chosen baseball instead,

and now, in 1961, at the age of 26, he was beginning his sixth season in the major leagues and his second with the Yankees. In manner he was polite, a little shy and dead honest; and by the curious logic of sports journalism that meant that he wasn't particularly good copy for interviews. Which suited Roger fine.

Roger hit his first home run of the '61 season in the Yankees' 10th game. No one paid much attention. But by mid-August everyone was paying attention, both to Maris and to Mantle, for Roger had by then hit 40 homers, Mickey had hit 39, and both were going at such a pace that they were clearly beginning to threaten Ruth's record of 60 home runs in a season.

Ever since the Bambino had set this record in 1927 only a handful of major league players had even approached it by hitting over 50 – something Ruth had done four times! Hack Wilson of the Cubs had hit 56 in 1930, to set the National League record. Both Jimmy Foxx of the Athletics and Hank Greenburg of the Tigers had hit 58; and Johnny Mize, Willie Mays and Mickey Mantle had hit in the low 50s.

Between 4 August and 26 August

Maris hit 10 more homers, thus gaining admittance to the rarified Over-50 Club with a total of 51. Mantle, with 48, was close behind, and the press, sensing that this was a race to break the record, began calling them the M&M Boys and deluged them with an inordinate amount of coverage. Ruth hero-worshippers, who hated the idea that the Great Man's record might ever be topped, became increasingly edgy and petulant, and one of them, none other than Ford Frick, the baseball commissioner, decided it was time to lengthen the odds a little. Since Ruth had hit his 60 in the old 154-game season, said Frick, his record could only be broken within that number of games. Anyone who broke the record in a game between numbers 154 and 162 would merely have an asterisk placed next to his name in the record book.

The country promptly split into pro- and anti-asterisk camps, just as it was already beginning to split into pro-Maris and pro-Mantle camps. In the latter contest, Mantle was plainly ahead. A 10-year Yankee veteran, already perceived as a superstar, fully at ease with the press, he was just the sort of man most people felt *should* break Ruth's record if it ever *had* to be broken. Whenever Mantle stepped onto the field people cheered him; now, whenever Maris stepped onto the field, people were beginning to boo him. So much for sportsmanship.

It got to the point where Mantle and Maris had to explain themselves to the press whenever they *didn't* hit a home run. After one such game against the Tigers, Mantle was constrained to point out that 'Mossi, their pitcher, had good stuff,' and Maris could only philosophize, 'When you're lousy, you're lousy.' By early September the pressure had gotten so acute that Maris's close-cropped blond hair was beginning to fall out in clumps.

Maris, at 58 home runs, was still ahead of Mantle when the Yankees played game number 154 against the Orioles in Baltimore on 20 September. The fact that this was Ruth's home town didn't make the fans' reception of Maris any warmer. Yet when, in the third inning, he hit homer number 59, for the first time Roger Maris was cheered on enemy turf. But he didn't make 60, and the asterisk won. 'I'm tired,' said Maris to the horde of reporters who besieged him in front of his locker after the game. 'I'm lucky to have hit as many as I did. I gave it my best shot, but I only got one.'

In Yankee Stadium on 26 September,

LEFT: *Mickey Mantle of the New York Yankees at bat in 1961.*

before a full house that included Babe Ruth's widow, Roger Maris became the second man in history to hit 60 home runs in a season. It happened in the third inning when Orioles pitcher Jack Fisher threw Maris a curve. 'I threw it, and the minute I did I said to myself that does it: That's 60,' recalled Fisher later. The crowd was on its feet roaring as Maris jogged around the bases. Mrs Ruth left her box and headed toward the exit, tears streaming from her eyes.

For the next three games Maris drew a blank, and thus he entered game 162, the last game of the season, still tied with Ruth. The game was to be played on 1 October, a Sunday, in Yankee Stadium against the Yankees' old rivals, the Boston Red Sox.

In his first time at bat Maris flied out to left. When he came up again in the third inning, the Red Sox pitcher, Tracy Stallings, determined not to become the answer to a trivia question, pitched Maris two balls. The crowd began to boo. The third pitch came at the plate about belt high, and suddenly Stallings, everyone in the stadium and millions of television viewers knew

that this was the moment. Maris swung and then stood watching as the ball soared out over right field. As he began his home run trot pandemonium overtook the stadium. The Yankees wouldn't let him into the dugout until he had received a long standing ovation, and then he was obliged to return for four curtain calls. The final score was Yankees – 1, Boston – 0. The great chase was at last over, and Roger Maris had hit more home runs in a season than any man.

Was his achievement greater than Ruth's? The matter will always be debated, but it is worth remembering that Ruth played only in the daylight, never had to change a time zone except when playing in Chicago or St Louis and, most important, never had to face a fraction of the psychological pressure inflicted on Maris. Still, this may be a case in which comparisons serve little purpose. Perhaps Maris put it best when he said to a friend: 'I don't understand it. There is only one Babe Ruth, and there's only one Mickey Mantle. All I wanted to be was Roger Maris.'

ABOVE: *Yankee slugger Roger Maris hits his record-breaking 61st home run in 1961.*
BELOW: *Maris displays some of the telegrams he received after setting his home run record.*

SANDY KOUFAX'S PERFECT GAME

In 1961, while the whole world watched Roger Maris in his pursuit of Babe Ruth's home run record, a young left-hander in Los Angeles was beginning to blossom as the Dodgers had hoped he might when they signed Sandy Koufax to a contract in 1955. Back then, under the bonus rules, a player who was signed for a certain amount of money couldn't be sent to the minor leagues. This was the situation that prevailed when Sandy Koufax joined another bonus baby named Don Drysdale on the Dodgers' bench. But since the team he joined was usually in some heated pennant race, rookies didn't get much chance to pitch, being mostly restricted to mopping up in the late innings of games that were not in question.

Blessed with outstanding athletic ability, as well as a blazing fastball, young Koufax had serious control problems, and his emergence as a great pitcher had taken a long time. But through a great deal of hard work Koufax had learned to control and spot his fastball and had developed a fine curve to go along with it. Starting in 1961, Koufax won 18 games and struck out 269 batters in 256 innings. In 1962, by the middle of the season, Koufax had a 14-5 record, and he threw his first no-hitter against the Mets on 30 June, 5-0. But then, suddenly, Koufax came down with a circulatory ailment in the fingers of his pitching hand. The pain was so great that he considered retirement, and for a time the doctors were afraid that amputation might be the only solution. But in the end treatments and rest finally relieved the problem.

In 1963 Koufax came back to lead the National League in pitching, striking out 306 and winning 25 games. He pitched his second no-hitter on 11 May, beating the San Francisco Giants 8-0. And in the World Series against the Yankees, Koufax won two, as the

Dodgers swept the Pinstripers in as stunning a performance as has been seen in the history of the Series. On 2 October 1953 Carl Erskine of the Dodgers had set a World Series strike-out record by fanning 14 New York Yankees. Ten years later to the day, in the first game of the Series, Sandy Koufax struck out 15.

On 4 June 1964 Koufax pitched his third no-hitter in three years, beating the Philadelphia Phillies, but the St Louis Cardinals won the National League pennant that year and went on to beat the New York Yankees, who had won their fifth American League pennant in a row.

In all the years that Sandy Koufax pitched for the Dodgers, he never really had a 'laugher,' a baseball term that means a game in which your teammates get you a big lead. When the Dodgers had great hitters like Snider,

ABOVE: *Dodger southpaw pitcher Sandy Koufax making a delivery to the plate.*

Hodges, Campanella and the others, Koufax was just learning to pitch. By the time he and Don Drysdale began to be winners, the Dodgers' offense was relatively weak, and most of their hitters were content with singles. Each time a Dodgers pitcher took the mound, he knew he would have to hold the other guys to under two runs.

By 1965 the Dodgers' only real weapon was the pitching of Koufax and Drysdale. Koufax won 26 and set the major league mark for strikeouts by fanning 382 batters. Drysdale won 23 games and struck out over 250 batters. On the night of 9 September, in Dodger Stadium, Sandy Koufax reached perfection and set a standard of pitching excellence that may never be matched.

The Dodgers were in a very tight pennant race with the Giants, and this night found them facing the Chicago Cubs, with one of the hardest-hitting batting orders in baseball. Ernie Banks, Ron Santo and Billy Williams were as good a trio of hitters as any team could hope to have, and pitching against Koufax was Bob Hendley, a fine left-hander. In a game the Dodgers had to win, Hendley was matching Koufax pitch for pitch. Only in the fifth inning did the Dodgers take the lead – in typical fashion, a run without a hit. Lou Johnson walked off Hendley and then was sacrificed to second. He stole third and came home to score when the Cubs catcher threw wildly to third.

The Dodgers still didn't have a hit off Hendley. But then, Chicago hadn't a hit off Koufax, and no Cub had reached first base. In the seventh, with two out,

RIGHT : *Hoosier pitcher Carl 'Oisk' Erskine of the Brooklyn/Los Angeles Dodgers. In the 1953 Series he struck out 14, including Mantle four times.*
BELOW: *Another view of the Dodgers' pitcher Sandy Koufax in action.*

Johnson blooped a double to right, and Henley lost his no-hitter, but the bloop was the only hit the Dodgers got. Nor did either team get a hit in the eighth. As Koufax walked to the mound in the top of the ninth he was well aware that the next few minutes could make baseball history.

The leadoff batter was the catcher, Chris Krug, whose error had given the Dodgers their only run. He struck out. Next was pinch-hitter Joey Amalfitano, a tough right-handed batter. He went down swinging. Now Koufax had to face another pinch-hitter, this time a former American League batting champ, Harvey Kuenn. Kuenn was past his prime, but as a right-handed hitter he was dangerous to southpaw Koufax. Three pitches, three swings and Sandy Koufax had his perfect game. He had faced 27 batters: Only seven got the ball to the outfield, 14 struck out, and six hit ground-outs.

The Dodgers won the National League pennant that year and beat the Minnesota Twins in the World Series. Koufax won the final game, striking out 10. By 1966 Sandy Koufax had to soak his arm in ice after each outing to reduce the swelling. He nevertheless won his second consecutive Cy Young Award, his third overall, as the best pitcher in baseball.

But the doctors had warned him that irreversible damage to his arm would result if he continued pitching, and in an emotional scene after the end of the season, Sandy Koufax announced his retirement. Between 1961 and 1966 he had won 111 games and lost only 34. He set the single season strikeout record and pitched four no-hitters, more than any other pitcher in history. He was not yet 30 years old when injuries forced his retirement.

THE RED SOX WIN THE PENNANT

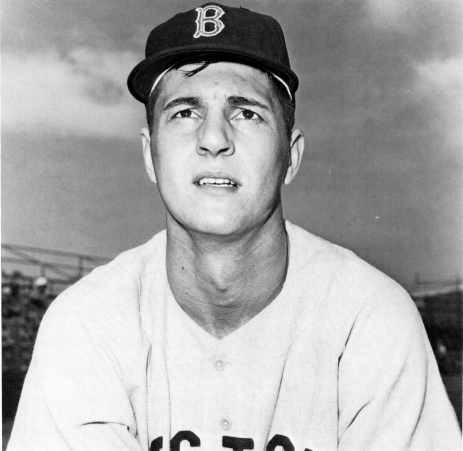

For most of the late 50s and throughout the 60s the Boston Red Sox were a second-division team. When they finished ninth in a 10-team league in 1966, the Red Sox management finally decided to do something about it. They hired a rookie manager named Dick Williams, and the demanding, acid-tongued Williams got the Red Sox moving.

When Ted Williams retired, the Sox had signed a young freshman from Notre Dame by way of Long Island. His name was Carl Yastrzemski, and the Sox said he'd make the fans forget about the Splendid Splinter. An excellent fielder with a deadly arm, Yaz, as he immediately became known, at first didn't make anyone forget about Williams when he batted. That was still in the future.

The favored teams for the American League pennant in 1967 were the Baltimore Orioles, the defending World Champions, the Detroit Tigers and the Minnesota Twins. The Yankees had fallen on bad times since their last pennant in 1964 and were not a factor. Neither were the Boston Red Sox, according to the experts. But baseball is a funny game and the experts are seldom right in their forecasts. The Orioles lost their great young pitcher, Jim Palmer, to injuries and eventually would finish sixth. The Tigers and Twins were still playing up to standard, but suddenly, from ninth place in 1966, along came the Boston Red Sox, carried by the bat of Carl Yastrzemski.

As it came down to the wire, the Red Sox and the Minnesota Twins met in Fenway Park for the last games of the season. The Twins had come to Boston with a one-game lead, but the Red Sox evened the race with a victory. Now it was a matter of one last game between the Twins and the Bosox. Detroit was also even with them and was now playing the California Angels. A Tigers win would thus produce a playoff between themselves and the winner in Fenway Park.

Red Sox ace Jim Lonborg, whose pitching had carried the Sox, faced a tough Minnesota team led by home run-hitting Harmon Killebrew. In the first inning, Lonborg got the first two Twins, but Killebrew walked. Now the leftfield wall, the famed 'Green Monster,' reached out and bit the Red Sox. Tony Oliva banked a line drive off the wall, and the ball bounced past Yaz and into center field. Reggie Smith

ABOVE LEFT: *Manager Dick Williams of the 1967 pennant-winning Boston Red Sox.*
LEFT: *Outfielder Carl Michael 'Yaz' Yastrzemski of the Red Sox.*

hits a bouncer over the mound. Second baseman Zoilo Versailles grabs it, and, instead of going to first, he fires home – too late, as Jones scores. Chance is out, and Al Worthington relieves. The first batter is George Scott, who squares around to bunt. Worthington wild pitches, and two Red Sox runners move up to second and third. Two more pitches and then Worthington throws another wild one, and Yaz scores. Scott finally strikes out, but the Red Sox now lead 4-2. Next Rico

---

LEFT: *Jim Lonborg, the star eight-handed pitcher for the Red Sox.*
BELOW: *George Scott douses Carl Yastrzemski with champagne after he clinched the pennant.*

Petrocelli walks, and Reggie Smith singles off Killebrew's glove, and the Red Sox score their fifth run.

Lonborg gives up a run in the eighth, but in the ninth he overpowers the Twins. And suddenly the Boston Red Sox, ninth in 1966, are the American League pennant winners in 1967. Carl Yastrzemski wins the Triple Crown, as he leads the league in hitting, at .321, and in RBI's, with 121, and he ties Harmon Killebrew in home runs, at 44. He is easily the Most Valuable Player in the American League. Although the Red Sox will lose the World Series to the Cardinals, the 1967 season will forever be remembered by Red Sox fans everywhere as 'The Impossible Dream' come true.

picked it up and threw home. George Scott cut off the throw, wheeled – and threw it into the screen behind home plate as Killebrew scored.

In the third, with two out, the Sox got hurt again. Lonborg walked Cesar Tovar, and then Killebrew singled to left. The ball bounced past Yastrzemski and rolled to the wall as Tovar came in for a 2-0 lead. The Boston fans were very quiet now, and when the scoreboard showed that the Tigers had lost to the Angels, everyone realized that the winner of this game would play the St Louis Cardinals in the World Series.

Dean Chance, the Twins pitcher, keeps the lid on the Sox for five innings, but in the sixth what happens will rank in Boston folklore right up there with the Brinks robbery. Lonborg gets on with a swinging bunt, and Jerry Adair lines a single past a diving Rod Carew at first. Then Dalton Jones, after fouling off a couple of pitches while trying to sacrifice, lines a single to left, loading the bases. The noise level in Fenway Park, which was ear-shattering when the game began, is now unbelievable.

Yastrzemski is the batter. He already has two hits today to go along with his homer and two singles yesterday. Now Yaz takes a ball and then lines Chance's next pitch to center for a single. Lonborg and Adair score and Fenway Park is rocking. Those are Yaz's 120th and 121st runs batted in, and probably the most important he has ever had.

The Boston fans have showered the field with streamers and paper cups, and through the debris, Ken Harrelson

1968: THE YEAR OF THE PITCHER

Every season in baseball has highlights that are memorable, but probably no single season presented so many outstanding pitching feats as the season of 1968. One statistic suggests how the pitchers dominated. Carl Yastrzemski won his second straight American League batting title that year. His average was just .301, the lowest in modern baseball history.

In 1964 Charlie Finley, owner of the Oakland Athletics, paid enough ($75,000) to get a young 18-year-old from North Carolina into an As' uniform, and the first year the As played in Oakland, Jim 'Catfish' Hunter pitched a perfect game. Not since 1921 had an American League pitcher hurled perfection in the regular season.

But Hunter was to pitch his masterpiece against the hard-hitting Minnesota Twins on 9 May 1968. A big man at 6ft 4in and 195 pounds, Hunter possessed good speed, had a fine curve and slider and had excellent control. Against the Twins, Hunter struck out 11, and only five balls were hit out of the infield. Hunter struck out Harmon Killebrew three times. He went to the

count of 3-0 to Tony Oliva in the second inning, and then struck out the two-time league batting leader. 'I just tried to strike out everybody; control is the name of the game,' Hunter said after the game.

Unlike many pitchers who throw no-hitters and fade into oblivion, Catfish Hunter would go on to win over 200 games in the majors. The nickname 'Catfish,' incidentally, came from Charlie Finley. Knowing little about North Carolina, he assumed Jim Hunter was a good old farm boy and must have fished for catfish when he was young. Hunter had never in fact fished for catfish or anything else, but it was a good public relations ploy, and the name stuck.

Down the coast in Los Angeles a pitcher who was half of one of the best duos in baseball history was working on breaking a mark that had stood for over 50 years. His name was Don Drysdale and, along with Sandy Koufax, he was the heart of the Dodgers teams that won World Series in 1963 and 1965. On the night of 9 June Drysdale faced the Philadelphia

Phillies. He had already hurled six consecutive shutouts, and he needed two more scoreless innings to tie the great Walter Johnson, who had set the record with 56 scoreless innings back in 1913. Drysdale tied the record when he held the Phillies scoreless in the first two innings and broke the Big Train's record when he shut them down in the third. The spell was finally broken when the Phillies pushed a run across in the last of the fifth inning, but by then Don Drysdale had set a new standard of excellence for pitchers by pitching 58⅔ scoreless innings.

At least as impressive was the accomplishment of Dennis Dale McLain of the Detroit Tigers. In 1968 Dennis McLain became the first American League pitcher to win 31 games since Lefty Grove did it for Connie Mack's Athletics back in 1931. And he became the first 30-game winner since Dizzy Dean did it in 1934.

Actually, it was the 30th win that

BELOW : *Jim 'Catfish' Hunter of the Oakland As pitching his perfect game against the Twins.*

ABOVE: *Don Drysdale of the Dodgers being interviewed by former teammate Sandy Koufax.*

captured the nation's fancy. Unlike Roger Maris's chase of the Babe Ruth record, McLain's attempt to become a 30-game winner was a more festive pursuit than the soul-searing ordeal that Maris went through. On 15 September, playing before a national television audience, and with Dizzy Dean in the crowd, McLain went for his 30th win against the young, strong Oakland As. McLain's pitching had carried the Tigers to within a few games of clinching the American League flag, but early in this game he seemed to be in trouble. In the third inning McLain gave up a two-run homer to Reggie Jackson, then just emerging as a feared slugger. But then Norm Cash got a three-run homer in the bottom of the fourth, and McLain had his lead back at 3-2.

He lost it again in the fifth when he gave up one run, and in the sixth, when with two outs, Jackson connected with a McLain fastball to give the As a 4-3 lead. In the eighth the Tigers got two men on. With two out, Gates Brown came up to bat. McLain was the next batter. If Brown got on, the Tigers would pinch-hit for McLain, and he'd

have no chance for his 30th. But Brown bounced out, and so McLain pitched in the ninth, breezing past the three Oakland hitters. Now the Tigers came to bat in their half of the ninth needing a run to tie and two to win.

Al Kaline, the great Tigers hitter, led off with a walk. The next batter fouled out, but Mickey Stanley grounded a single through the box, and Kaline hustled to third. With the infield in to cut off the tying run, Jim Northrup, the Tigers' hitter, bounced the ball to first. The As' first baseman had an easy play at home, but he threw it high, and Kaline slid under the tag, safe. The game was tied.

Because the Tigers had a man on third and first, with only one out, the As had to play the infield in to cut off the run in case of a ground ball. Similarly, the outfield had to come in also, so as to have a chance of throwing out the runner on a fly ball. Willie Horton, one of the Tigers' strongest hitters, went to a count of 2-2 and then hit a long fly to left, over the head of the pulled-in outfielder. As the ball went over the fielder's head, McLain raced over to home to hug his teammates. They in turn carried him around the field in a crush of fans, sportswriters and photographers.

While Denny McLain was winning his 31 games, the dominant pitcher in the National League was Bob Gibson of the St Louis Cardinals. In 1968 this tall, hard-throwing right-hander pitched the Redbirds to their second consecutive National League flag, winning 22 games and losing but nine. He won the league's MVP and Cy Young awards, and when the Detroit Tigers won the American League flag, all of baseball looked forward to the pitching duel between the two leading pitchers in their respective leagues.

The 'pitching duel of the century' ended in the fourth inning of Game One. Gibson struck out seven of the first nine Tigers who faced him. He got Al Kaline on a third called strike and then sat in the dugout as his teammates got to Denny McLain. Two walks, a single and a double by Mike Shannon gave Gibson all the runs he would need as the Redbirds scored three times. Now the brilliant flame-thrower began his assault on the strikeout record set by Sandy Koufax. By the end of the eighth inning he was only one behind Koufax's 15.

Mickey Stanley, who later would play a major role in the final outcome of the Series, gave Gibson a blow by opening the ninth with a single. But Al

Kaline went down swinging, and the scoreboard flashed '15.' Norm Cash did the same on the first three pitches Gibson threw, and Bob Gibson was the new strikeout King of World Series play. When William Horton took strike three to end the game, Gibson's new standard jumped to 17.

While the world was applauding Gibson the Series continued. The Tigers rebounded 8-1 behind the pitching of left-hander Mickey Lolich, who had toiled throughout the season in relative obscurity behind the dazzling McLain. The Cardinals won Game Three in Detroit, and in Game Four Bob Gibson won again 10-1. Trailing the Cardinals three games to one, the Tigers battled back and won Game Five, Lolich picking up his second win. The Series then shifted to St Louis, and the Tigers, behind Denny McLain, won Game Six 13-1, thus tying the Series.

In Game Seven the Tigers had to face Bob Gibson. Working with just two days rest, Mickey Lolich was to handle the pitching chores for Detroit. Both he and Gibson had won two games in the Series, and Gibson was working on his seventh consecutive World Series victory.

He seemed to be well on his way to making it, retiring the first 10 Tigers, before Mickey Stanley got him for an infield single. But then Gibson got another 10 in a row, striking out six and breaking the all-time strikeout record for a World Series. In the meantime,

OPPOSITE: *Detroit pitcher Denny McLain.*
BOTTOM: *Mickey Lolich of the Detroit Tigers.*
BELOW: *Bob Gibson, the intimidating pitcher for the St Louis Cardinals.*

however, Lolich was quietly keeping the Cardinals from scoring.

Going into the seventh, still scoreless, Gibson struck out Stanley, and Kaline grounded out. Suddenly, the Tigers came alive. With two out, Norm Cash singled to right, and Willie Horton bounced a ball through the infield for a single. Next, Jim Northrup lofted a long fly to deep left center, apparently an easy third out for the skilled Curt Flood, the Cardinals' star centerfielder. But Flood misjudged the catch, and when he turned to chase the ball he tripped and fell. Two Tigers scored, and when Bill Freehan singled, Northrup scored from third. The Tigers had broken Bob Gibson and led 3-0.

Mickey Lolich gave the Cardinals only one run, a home run in the ninth, and the Tigers, coming from two games down, won the 1968 World Series. The hero was not the great Bob Gibson, who, but for Flood's error, might have won a record seventh consecutive game. Nor was it the fabulous Denny McLain. It was the unsung Mickey Lolich, who became the first left-handed pitcher to win three games in a World Series, who won the award as the Series' Most Valuable Player and who thus ended the season that richly deserves the title 'Year of The Pitcher.'

THE AMAZIN' METS

When Walter O'Malley's Dodgers and Horace Stoneham's Giants raced west to mine the golden ores of California, the National League had to replace those two teams in the biggest media market in the country. Thus in 1962 the New York Mets were whelped, and that season they helped bring back slapstick humor to the game, for the Mets of Casey Stengel couldn't hit, run, throw, catch or pitch.

Stocked with unwanted players from the other National League teams, the Mets entertained the rest of the National League in their maiden season by losing 120 games. Now that the National League was a 10-team league, the Mets were able to finish 10th for four straight years. In 1966 they moved up to ninth, where they also ended up in 1968. There was therefore no reason, as the 1969 season began, not to pencil in the Mets as ninth- or 10th-place finishers.

But changes were quietly being made. Casey Stengel had retired and had been replaced by the Brooklyn

Dodgers hero, Gil Hodges. A gentleman, Hodges nevertheless was a strict disciplinarian. He was used to winning and brought that expectation to the Mets. The Mets' consistent last-place finishes put them high in the baseball draft, and under Hodges they began to build the nucleus of a solid pitching staff. The prize of the staff was a bright, articulate athlete from Southern California named Tom Seaver. Seaver had originally signed with the Atlanta Braves (the ex-Milwaukee Braves, who had abandoned Sudsville when Atlanta made them a better offer). But the Braves had paid Seaver a bonus for signing, and, under a technicality, the commissioner ruled that the Braves had to give up Seaver. At the commissioner's office those teams interested in the young pitcher could put their names in a hat, and the team drawn first could bid for Tom Seaver. The Mets' scrap of paper came out first, and Tom Seaver became a New York Met. So much for scouting and drafting.

Joining Seaver were left-hander Jerry Koosman, a 17-game winner, Nolan Ryan, the fastest pitcher in baseball, and Tug McGraw. A good staff, but in Las Vegas, before the season began, the odds-makers' line on the National League season had the Cardinals, the defending champions, at 5-1 and the Mets at 100-1.

ABOVE: *Pitcher Tom Seaver – the star of the Amazin' Mets.*
BELOW: *The 1969 World Series-winning New York Mets.*

in Game Two, Jerry Koosman out-pitched Dave McNally and won 2-1. Now, as the Series went to Shea Stadium, Earl Weaver, the cocky Orioles manager, insisted the Koosman victory would be the only one the Mets would get. He was wrong. Tommy Agee made two catches off long drives to preserve Gary Gentry's 5-0 victory. Next Seaver got his chance to pick up a win, and he did just that, with a sparkling 2-1 victory. Now the Mets led three games to one, with the fifth to be played at Shea Stadium. So far, it seemed, everything the Orioles hit a Met had caught, whereas the Mets' little dribblers or pop-ups always seemed to stay fair or to have eyes. The Orioles' frustration was obvious. They knew they were the better team. But the Mets had to be shown.

The fifth game pits Jerry Koosman against Dave McNally. McNally is one of the better-hitting pitchers in base-ball, while Koosman has a mere four singles to show in 84 at bats. The first two innings are scoreless, but in the third the powerful Orioles finally show the power that has made them the most feared team in the American League. Mark Belanger, their fine shortstop, singles to open the third. That brings up the pitcher, McNally, who promptly smashes a Koosman pitch into the left-field bullpen. Two outs later, Frank Robinson hits Koosman's first pitch over the centerfield wall, and the Orioles have a three-run lead. The Mets seem to have run out of miracles.

After the rough third inning, Koosman settles down and keeps the Orioles at bay. But McNally is doing

LEFT: ;*Pitcher Dave McNally hits a two-run homer for the Orioles in the Series.*
BELOW: *Mike Cuellar, the star southpaw of the Baltimore Orioles.*

Because the National League had expanded into Montréal and San Diego, the league split into two divisions, East and West. The Mets were in the Eastern Division, with Philadelphia, St Louis, Chicago, Pittsburgh and Montréal.

By September Seaver and Koosman had, together, won 19 games and finished eight games ahead of the Chicago Cubs, who had out-hit and out-scored the Mets in every category. Tommy Agee led the Mets with 75 RBI's, 26th best in the National League. It didn't matter; the Mets were 'Destiny's Darlings.' They met the Atlanta Braves in the first National League playoff. The Braves were led by Henry Aaron, who had hit 44 home runs in '69, and knuckleballer Phil Nekro, who had 23 wins. It didn't matter; the Mets swept the best-of-five series. Now on to the World Series.

The team the Mets would face was the Baltimore Orioles. They were considered by most to be the greatest American League team since the 1961 Yankees, and many said they were even better. They had won the Eastern Division by 19 games over the Tigers. Boog Powell, Frank Robinson, Paul Blair and Brooks Robinson had hit 118 homers among them, but even more impressive was the Orioles' pitching, for Jim Palmer, Mike Cuellar and Dave McNally had won 60 games among them. 'Orioles, easy, in four; five, no more,' was the word in Vegas and along press row.

Sure enough, in the first game the Orioles beat Seaver and the Mets 4-1, with Mike Cuellar getting the win. But

the same. Then, in the top of the sixth, Oriole Frank Robinson is hit by a pitch, but the umpire, Lou DiMuro, rules that the ball hit the bat first and is a foul ball. Earl Weaver is livid and is screaming at DiMuro. Robinson goes into the dugout to have some ice put on his bruise, and when he comes back on the field, the Mets fans are standing waving handkerchiefs at the Orioles' star. He strikes out on the next pitch.

In the Mets' half of the sixth, when Cleon Jones is batting, a McNally curve dips down and in, hitting him on the instep. The umpire calls it a ball, but Jones insists he was hit. Remembering the 'look-at-the-ball trick,' Gil Hodges retrieves the ball from the Mets' dugout, where it had bounced. Showing the spot of shoe polish on the ball to DiMuro, Hodges watches with a poker face as the umpire reverses his call and

LEFT: *Jerry Koosman of the strong New York Mets pitching staff.*
BELOW: *New York fans run wild after their Mets have won the Series.*

ABOVE: *Met manager Gil Hodges get a celebratory bath in champagne from Jerry Koosman.*

sends Jones to first. Weaver is out on the field like a shot, screaming, the veins in his neck bulging, his face flushed. But he loses the argument, and Jones stays on first. The next hitter is Don Clendenon, who has already hit two home runs in the Series. He goes to two and two with McNally and then smashes a drive off the auxiliary scoreboard on the facing of the leftfield loge seats. Now the Mets trail 3-2. In the seventh Koosman again keeps the Orioles from crossing home plate, and in the Mets' half, little Al Weis belts McNally's second pitch over the 371-ft mark in left center. Mets – 3, Orioles – 3.

In the eighth, with Eddie Watt pitching for McNally, Cleon Jones lines a double to left. Donn Clendenon bounces out, and Ron Swoboda comes to bat. He doubles down the leftfield line, with Jones coming across with the lead run. Ed Charles flies out to center, but catcher Jerry Grote lines a ball low to the ground towards Boog Powell, the first baseman. The huge Powell can't get the handle on the ball and boots it, chases it and throws to Watt, covering first. Watt juggles the throw and then drops it, as the hustling Swoboda flashes across home plate with the Mets' fifth run.

Going into the ninth, the Orioles' Frank Robinson quiets Shea Stadium with a walk, for with Powell and Brooks Robinson coming up, there is still enough time for the Orioles. But Powell forces Frank Robinson at second with a grounder, and then Brooks Robinson flies out to Swoboda. Now Koosman faces Davy Johnson, the Orioles' second baseman, who has plenty of power to tie up the game with one swing. But Koosman gets him to hit a fly ball to left center, and when Cleon Jones squeezes the ball, Shea Stadium explodes.

Nothing is safe from fans suddenly gone mad. Bases are ripped up, the pitchers' mound is pulled from the hooks holding it down. Grown men and children fight over patches of turf, and in almost no time the playing field looks like a dust bowl. Firecrackers explode, graffiti appears on the bleacher walls and people are trying to rip the seats from the grandstands.

Joe DiMaggio, who threw out the honorary first ball, stands in his box by the Mets dugout, watching in disbelief. 'I never saw anything like this,' he exclaims. But of course nobody had ever seen anything like the Amazin' Mets, now, incredibly, the champions of all baseball.

HENRY AARON HITS NUMBER 715

In a box score from a baseball game played on 23 April 1954 a notation at the bottom read, 'Home runs: Milwaukee; Aaron (1).' Unless you were a big Braves fan, that brief notation of Henry Aaron's first home run would have meant little, for Aaron arrived in the major leagues without fanfare. Nor, even after he had been playing for the Braves for a while, did recognition come quickly. Unlike the colorful and flamboyant Willie Mays, Aaron was a solid player, always there, quietly doing his job. It took years before the nation's press recognized how great were Aaron's skills.

Aaron's swing was compact, efficient and deadly. A wrist hitter, he would wait until the last second before whipping his bat into the ball, and he sprayed his line drives to all fields. As he matured, he began hitting more home runs each year. He and Mays both led the National League in homers four times, and Aaron also led his league in runs batted in four times. On 27 April 1971 Henry Aaron hit his 600th home run, joining Babe Ruth and Willie Mays as the only players in baseball history to hit over 600 home runs in a career.

Most experts had now come to rank

Henry Aaron as one of the greatest all-round players in the history of the game, but none thought he or Mays would ever break the Babe's lifetime home run record of 714. The experts were correct about Mays, for the Giants' great was on the last leg of his fabulous career. Aaron still had a shot, but he knew he had to average better than 30 home runs a season to get to Ruth.

Incredibly, he did, and as the baseball season of 1973 came to an end, Henry Aaron had 713 home runs. He had smashed 40 homers that season but had run out of games. All of sports now waited for Opening Day of 1974 and the inevitable toppling of the Babe's record.

The Milwaukee Braves had been drawing over a million fans a year when Lou Perini sold them to a combine headed by Bill Bartholomay. Al-

BELOW: *Henry 'Hank' Aaron of the Braves in the 1958 World Series.*

ABOVE: *Aaron hitting his 715th homer against the Dodgers – 8 April 1974.*
RIGHT: *Baseball Commissioner Bowie Kuhn, who ordered the Braves to play Aaron in Cincinnati.*

though he had promised to keep the Braves in Milwaukee, Bartholomay let out the word that he'd move the Braves to another city for a better deal. Atlanta built him a stadium, and Bartholomay headed south in 1966. When the 1974 schedule for the National League was published, the Braves were scheduled to open the season in Cincinnati, play-ing their first three games there. Claim-ing he was doing it for the Atlanta fans, Bartholomay had ordered Henry not to play in those games. A less generous interpretation of this decision might have been that if Aaron broke the record in Cincinnati, the crowd, and therefore the gate, for the Braves' opener in Atlanta would be much smaller. In any case, with a real under-standing of the essence of sport, Bartholomay had issued his order during the winter, long before the '74 season began. This gave plenty of time for acrimonious, and often unseemly,

ABOVE: *Aaron (left) scores after hitting his 715th homer.*
BELOW: *Al Downing, the Dodger pitcher who gave up the record-setting homer.*

controversy to develop among fans and in the press, but it also gave the commissioner time to intervene. Bowie

Kuhn was often accused as being a tool of the owners, but Kuhn this time did the right thing, calling for Aaron to play in the Cincinnati opener if physically able.

On Opening Day Henry Aaron ended the controversy by smashing a home run in his first time at bat. He now had 714, tying the Babe. Without objection from Kuhn, Bartholomay now got his way and Aaron sat out the next two games in Cincinnati. Kuhn's feeling for baseball propriety apparently extended only to one game.

In front of the largest crowd in Atlanta history and a huge national television audience, Henry Aaron and the Braves faced the Los Angeles Dodgers. Pitching for the Dodgers was Al Downing, a former New York Yankee, who had no intention of joining the list of pitchers who gave up record-breaking home runs. When Aaron came to bat in the last of the first, Downing took no chances, walking Hank in five pitches. A few moments later Aaron scored on a double by teammate Dusty

Baker. With all the hoopla about Ruth's record, little attention was paid to the fact that as Hank Aaron touched home plate he set a National League record for most runs scored: 2063.

In the fourth, with the Dodgers leading 3-1, rain begins to fall on Fulton County stadium. Colorful umbrellas open, and the fans roar as Aaron walks to the batters' box. Downing's first pitch is a ball. Aaron watches without expression. Now Downing throws, and Aaron swings for the first time in the game. The ball rises high toward left center as the crowd comes to its feet. Deep and far the ball goes, into the Braves' bullpen. Skyrockets go off and the scoreboard lights flash '715.'

He jogs around the bases, and Dodgers infielders shake his hand. As he heads towards his waiting teammates a man bolts out from a special box. It is Hank's 65-year-old father, Herbert Aaron. He is first at home plate to shake the hand of the man who broke the great Babe Ruth's lifetime home run record.

FISK'S HOME RUN IN THE 1979 SERIES

The World Series that the Red Sox and Reds played in 1975 has become known as one of the most exciting in baseball history. Going into the Series, the Reds were favored to win their first title in 35 years. This team was called 'the Big Red Machine,' and it truly was one of the greatest teams ever put together. Eight starters had played together for two pennant seasons, and five of the hitters batted over .300. Their lineup may some day be all together in the Hall of Fame. Pete Rose at third, Joe Morgan at second, Tony Perez at first and Jose Concepion at short made up one of the best National League infields of all time. Add Ken Griffey, George Foster and Cesar Geronimo in the outfield, and you have a super cast to support any pitcher. But the key to the Reds was their catcher. Not since Roy Campanella and Yogi Berra were catching for the Dodgers and Yankees respectively had baseball seen a catcher as gifted as Johnny Bench. Blessed with a powerful, accurate throwing arm, Bench was a great student of the game and had a sixth

ABOVE: *The Cincinnati Reds' all-star catcher, Johnny Bench, behind the plate.* LEFT: *Pete Rose – 'Charlie Hustle' – of the Cincinnati Reds.*

sense about base stealers, and his catching instincts brought many a Reds pitcher to victory. He also hit both for power and averages, twice leading the league in home runs and three times in runs batted in. When Ted Williams was introduced to Bench after Johnny had first come up to the big leagues, Bench asked the great slugger to autograph a baseball to him. Williams signed it 'To Johnny Bench, a future Hall of Famer.'

The pitching staff that was the beneficiary of all this talent did not have a 20-game winner among them. The reason was manager Sparky Anderson. Anderson's pitching philosophy was simple: Have your starter throw as hard as he can from the first inning, and when he tires, bring in more hard throwers from the bullpen. Because he had such men in the pen, the strategy worked, but it didn't hurt also to have the hardest-hitting team in baseball.

Against the Big Red Machine the Red Sox threw their own exceptional players. They were still led by Carl Yastrzemski, with Dwight Evans, Carlton Fisk and Cecil Cooper forming a hardy back-up group of hitters. In 1975 the Red Sox had also come up with a pair of rookies who were the envy of all baseball: Jim Rice, a strong, hard-hitting outfielder and Fred Lynn, a marvelous fielder and hitter. Rice hit .309 and drove in 102 runs, while the graceful Lynn hit .331 and was the first player in baseball history to be named simultaneously the Rookie of the Year and the Most Valuable Player. The Red Sox pitching was led by the veteran Rick Wise and the entertaining and unpredictable Bill Lee. Added to that group was a grizzled, cigar-smoking old timer named Luis Tiant, who was easily the big comeback story of 1975.

The Series opened in Boston's Fenway Park. With the Green Monster in left field easily reachable by all the powerful, right-handed Cincinnati hitters, many thought these games would be slugfests. To the chant of 'Looie, Looie,' Tiant held the Big Red Machine scoreless as the Sox blanked the Reds 6-0. Game Two and Game Three belonged to the Reds 3-2 and 6-5. Tiant stopped the Reds in Cincy 5-4, and the Reds took a three-games-to-two lead, winning the pivotal fifth game 6-2. Now the Series moved to Boston for the last two games, with the Reds needing only one victory to win their first World Series since 1940.

The weather in Boston turned bad and for three days even commissioner Bowie Kuhn, who had attended these cold night games wearing long underwear under his pinstripe suit, couldn't do anything about the rains that swept in from Massachusetts Bay. Finally, on the night of 21 October, the weather relented, and Game Six was to be played.

Tiant put the Reds down in their half of the first. In the Sox half, after two out, Yaz singled to right, and Fisk followed that with a single to center. Still with two out, up stepped Fred Lynn

LEFT: *Right-handed pitcher Luis Tiant of the Boston Red Sox.*
BELOW: *The Red Sox Fred Lynn batting in the 1975 World Series – catching is Johnny Bench.*

ABOVE: *Boston Red Sox catcher Carlton Fisk at bat.*

Tiant continued to pitch brilliantly, holding the Reds scoreless in the sixth. But in the seventh they finally got to him when George Foster lined a long drive into center field that scored Griffey and Morgan. Sox manager Dick Williams immediately pulled Tiant, and as he walked from the mound the fans, chanting 'Looie, Looie,' gave him a standing ovation. In the top of the eighth the Reds scored again. Now they were leading 6-3 and were only six outs away from their predicted World Championship.

But the Red Sox won't quit. In their half of the eighth they get two men on, and with two outs, they call on pinch-hitter Bernie Carbo to hit. Trying not to strike out, Carbo leans into Rawley Eastwick's pitch and drives it into the right centerfield bleachers, tying the game. The old ball park on Kenmore Square shakes as the faithful roar in wave after wave of thunderous cheers.

In the ninth the Red Sox load up the bases, but a double play keeps them from winning. Into extra innings. In the eleventh Dwight Evans nabs a Joe Morgan drive into the gap in right center, and his throw doubles up the Reds' runner and gets the Red Sox out of trouble. As Pete Rose comes to bat at the start of the twelfth, he turns to Carlton Fisk, the Sox catcher, and says, 'This is some kind of game, isn't it?' Fisk replies, 'Some kind of game.'

In the Sox half of the twelfth, Carlton Fisk comes to bat with the score still tied 6-6. Fisk, a Vermonter, is one of the most popular of the recent Red Sox. Now, as he steps in to face Pat Darcy, the fans begin their rhythmic clapping, almost as much to shake off their exhaustion as much as to encourage Fisk. Darcy throws and Fisk swings, and as the ball flies into the New England darkness 34,000 eyes peer down the foul line towards the Green Monster and the foul pole. Everyone knows it has the distance; the only question is: Will it be fair? The ball smacks the screen along the foul pole . . . and bounces into the net over the fence. *Fair*! All hell breaks loose. Fans pour over the walls and run onto the field, and the security guards let them go.

Reds manager Sparky Anderson spoke to the press after the game: 'The way I hurt all over, it probably was as good a ballgame as I've ever seen. A great game in a great Series.'

In Game Seven, the Cincinnati Reds beat the Boston Red Sox 4-3, finally putting down the stubborn Sox as they won their first World Series in 35 years. But for Carlton Fisk, Dwight Evans, Luis Tiant and the rest of the Boston Red Sox, Game Six of the 1975 World Series will forever be 'the greatest game ever played.'

and smashed Gary Nolan's pitch to deep center field for a three-run homer.

But the Reds weren't called the Big Red Machine for nothing, and in the top of the fifth a walk and a single by Pete Rose put Reds on first and third. On a 2-2 pitch, Ken Griffey lined a pitch deep to center field. Centerfielder Lynn was off at the crack of the bat, and he and the ball met at the 379-ft mark

on the concrete centerfield fence. Lynn slumped to the ground as the ball rolled towards right field, and the two Reds runners scored, with Griffey ending up on third.

It took five minutes to revive the injured Lynn, but after he had walked around a bit he stayed in the game. Joe Morgan popped out for the second out of the inning, but Johnny Bench, whom Tiant had struck out twice, lined Tiant's first pitch off the leftfield wall, and Griffey scored, tying the game at three all.

Jackson's Three Consecutive Homers

In 1977 free agency became a reality in baseball, and all the horror stories the owners had predicted came true because the owners started hitting each other over the head with their bank accounts, bidding unbelievable dollars for the services of players who were free agents. Soon utility players were making three or four times what Musial, DiMaggio, Feller and Williams had made. The biggest stars were now offered seven-figure numbers, and the worst offender was the loudest critic of free agency, George Steinbrenner.

Steinbrenner and a group of investors had bought the New York Yankees from the Columbia Broadcasting System. Vowing to bring New York a pennant, Steinbrenner hired controversial Billy Martin to manage his team. In Steinbrenner, Billy Martin was working for an owner who knew a little about baseball but thought he knew more than any one in the game. In Martin, Steinbrenner had hired a man who knew baseball as well as any field manager in the game but couldn't get along with management. The two had egos the size of the Grand Canyon. And in 1977 they were joined by another ego every bit as big as theirs, that of Reginald Martinez Jackson.

Yankees pitcher Ken Holtzman had been a teammate of Reggie Jackson in Oakland. When asked by another Yankee what Jackson was like, he replied, 'You're not going to believe the bullshit.' When Jackson arrived at spring training, Holtzman's forecast was fully realized. Jackson immediately alienated Thurman Munson, the team captain, by proclaiming that he, Reggie Jackson, was the straw that stirred the drink and that he had an IQ

as big as his slugging percentage. One way or another, he soon totally dominated the Yankees' spring training.

Martin and Jackson of course clashed throughout the season, but if Jackson had a huge ego, he also had the talent to back it up. He hit 32 homers for the Yankees, and, along with Graig Nettles, Munson and Chris Chambliss, he helped the Yankees return to the powerhouse days of Mantle and Maris. He called himself Mr October, and in

TOP RIGHT: *Manager Billy Martin of the New York Yankees in the dugout.*
BELOW: *Catcher Thurman Munson of the Yankees tags Dodger Steve Garvey in the Series opener.*

ABOVE: *Reggie Jackson, the Yankee outfielder, taking a cut.*

the 1977 World Series, Reggie Jackson backed up that boast too.

The team the Yankees met in the Series was the Los Angeles Dodgers. Since they had gone west, the Dodgers had played in five World Series and won three. All that time they had been managed by Walter Alston, but now, after 23 years, he had retired and had been replaced by his coach, Tom Lasorda, who had been in the Dodgers system so long he claimed he 'bled Dodgers blue.' The team he brought to the Series was a youthful group that would stay together for almost a decade.

The teams split the first two games at Yankee Stadium, and the Yankees took two out of three at Chavez Ravine. The sixth game was played at Yankee Stadium. The Yankees took the field behind Mike Torrez, who had been the Yankees' top pitcher down the stretch and had won Game Three. The Dodgers jumped off to a 2-0 lead in the first. In the bottom of the second, Jackson led off with a walk and came home as Chris Chambliss homered to tie the game. The Dodgers took the lead 3-2, in the third, and it stood that way briefly until the Yankees' fifth. Munson singled, and Jackson hammered Burt Hooton's first pitch into the rightfield stands. In the sixth, Mickey Rivers singled, and after Randolph and Munson were put out, Reggie Jackson came to bat.

RIGHT: *Yankee owner George Steinbrenner hugs winning pitcher Mike Torrez.*
BELOW: *Reggie Jackson hugs his father after the Yankees won the World Series.*

Pitching for the Dodgers is Elias Sosa, who has replaced Burt Hooton. His first pitch is smashed by Jackson into the rightfield stands, up in the $15 seats, and the Yankees lead 7-3. Lasorda and the Dodgers are indeed bleeding Dodgers blue.

In the eighth Jackson comes to bat to a standing ovation from the Bronx faithful. Jackson stands just outside the batters' box savoring the applause as it rolls around Yankee Stadium. Taking his stance, with a few swings to loosen up, Jackson again hits the first pitch thrown. The ball jumps off his bat and flies deep to center field, 450 feet away. With this massive home run Reggie Jackson becomes the first batter to hit three home runs in a World Series game since Babe Ruth did it for the Yankees in 1926 and 1928. But not even the great Bambino had hit five home runs in a Series, as Jackson now has in this one, and to make Jackson's feat more outstanding, counting his last home run in Game Five, he has hit four home runs in a row, all on the first pitch.

The turmoil of the season and bruised egos are forgotten in the celebrating Yankees locker room. Billy Martin tells everyone that 'Reggie is sensational,' and George Steinbrenner is all smiles as he hugs Jackson and Martin. Reggie is Mr Modesty. 'Babe Ruth is great; I'm just lucky,' he says shyly. 'I'm so happy for George Steinbrenner, who stuck his neck out for me.'

To keep things in perspective in the Bronx Zoo, when Chris Chambliss is later asked if he thinks things will now be calmer after all the turmoil of the '77 season, he replies, 'I really doubt it.'

DENT'S HOMER IN THE 1978 PLAYOFF

As Cris Chambliss had so accurately predicted, the turmoil at Yankee Stadium didn't subside. If anything, it got worse in 1978.

Billy Martin and Reggie Jackson couldn't stand each other, and both of them were fighting for the attention of the New York press. Martin was also suffering from the constant criticism of the owner, George Steinbrenner, who wasn't happy that the Red Sox were the American League frontrunners. He wouldn't let Martin alone, publicly criticizing the players and their manager in the papers and not hesitating to pick up the phone in his office and call Martin on the bench in the middle of a game.

The New York press had a ball with the antics in the Bronx, and famed columnist Red Smith took to calling Steinbrenner 'George III.' It couldn't go on. When Martin and Jackson got into an argument on the bench, and a national television audience watched a manager and player almost come to blows, Steinbrenner managed to make matters worse by siding with Jackson while approving Martin's five-day suspension of the slugger.

When Billy Martin, not usually a funny man, heard about Steinbrenner's siding with Jackson, he cracked 'They deserve each other: One is a confirmed liar, and the other is a convicted liar.' (He was referring to the fact that Steinbrenner had lied under oath about money given to the Nixon presidential campaign and had been fined $10,000 and given a suspended sentence.)

When Martin's comment got back to George, he fired Martin (although he insisted Billy had resigned) and replaced him with Bob Lemon, a Hall of Fame pitcher who was the complete antithesis of Martin. Under his easy reign, the Yankees came alive, and, led by Ron Guidry's pitching and Jackson's slugging, the Yankees caught up to the Red Sox on the last day of the season, both having 99-63 records.

Often in playoff and World Series games, the heroes are players who are not the big stars of the teams. Harry Walker of the Cardinals in 1946, Dusty Rhodes of the Giants in 1951, Billy Martin of the Yankees and Moe Drabowski of the Orioles come to mind. In the Red Sox-Yankees playoff game, a good-field no-hit shortstop named Bucky Dent would make the difference for the Yankees.

The Yankees had picked up Dent from the Chicago White Sox through free agency. He was a dependable,

LEFT: *The New York Yankees slick-fielding shortstop, Bucky Dent.*

solid-fielding shortstop and blended
in nicely with the brilliant third baseman, Graig Nettles. Dent wasn't a
long-ball hitter, but through the season
he had delivered some key hits. And in
Fenway Park, where the playoff was to
take place, you didn't need to be a
fence buster to hit a home run over the
Green Monster, the nickname for the
leftfield wall.

The Red Sox jumped off to a three-
run lead, and going into the eighth
they led 4-1. But then the Yankees
rallied, and with two out, they had two
men on when Dent came to bat. Since
the American League had the desig-
nated hitter rule, Dent was the
Yankees' last batter in the lineup. So
the Sox had to get Dent out before they
faced the top of the Yankees' line-up.

Bucky Dent hit a long fly ball towards the leftfield fence. As the ball
soared towards the Green Monster, it
gradually became apparent that the
ball might clear the wall, and when it
did, sailing over the top of the fence
and landing in the screen behind the
wall, Bucky Dent joined the historic
legion of Yankees who had once again
killed the hopes of the Boston Red Sox.
Even though the score was still tied,

even diehard Red Sox fans somehow
knew that all was lost. When Reggie
Jackson hit a home run in the next
inning to win the game, the continuing
story of Red Sox failures had a new
chapter, written less by Jackson than
by Bucky Dent.

The Yankees went on to defeat the
Kansas City Royals again, for their
third American League title in a row,
even though George Brett of the Royals
hit three home runs. They then took
their second straight World Series from
the Los Angeles Dodgers.

Dent's homer in the Red Sox game
may have been one of the single
greatest moments in the 1978 season,
but overall, the season's hero was
probably another Yankee. In both the
playoffs and the World Series, the play
of Graig Nettles reminded viewers of
the great play that Brooks Robinson
had shown in the 1970 Series. Nettles
clearly established himself as one of
the great third basemen of his time. He
hit for power also, leading the league in
homers in 1976. But it was Nettles's
great diving stabs of sure base hits that
had the fans gasping, and three times
in the World Series, Nettles's great
plays stopped Dodgers' rallies.

ABOVE: *Third baseman Graig Nettles spears another shot.*
OPPOSITE: *Southpaw pitcher Ron Guidry of the New York Yankees.*
BELOW: *George Brett, the power-hitting third baseman of the Kansas City Royals.*

THE SEVENTH GAME IN THE 1979 SERIES

They called him 'Pops,' and he called them the 'Family,' and in 1979 Willie Stargell and the Pittsburgh Pirates family brought delighted smiles to baseball fans everywhere when they came back from two games down, with three to go, and defeated the Baltimore Orioles in the World Series.

In 1971 the Pirates had defeated these same Baltimore Orioles in a Series where the Orioles had been heavily favored. Back then the Pirates had been led by the brilliant Roberto Clemente, who hit two homers. And back then, in the seventh and final game, Willie Stargell had scored the winning run as the Pirates won 2-1.

Now, eight years later, the same two teams met again. The Orioles had replaced the Yankees as champions of the American League and featured strong pitching by Jim Palmer and Mike Flanagan, plus the hitting of Ken Singleton, Eddie Murray and Gary Roenicke. The Pirates had replaced the Dodgers atop the National League, having beaten the Reds in the league playoffs.

Stargell led the Pirates' hitters with

BELOW: *Willie 'Pops' Stargell, the great first baseman of the Pittsburgh Pirates.*

Willie
Stargell
8

32 home runs and was named co-MVP of the National League with Keith Hernandez of the St Louis Cardinals, who won the league batting title by hitting .344. The Pirates didn't have the front-line pitching to match Baltimore, but they had, in relief pitcher Kent Tekulve, the best answer to a call for help in baseball. The sidearm Tekulve had carried the Pirates with save after save during the pennant drive, and in the World Series he would prove his value again.

Baltimore took the Series opener; Pittsburgh narrowly won the second; and then the Orioles, behind heavy hitting, bounced back to take the next two in a row. The Pirates staved off elimination by winning the fifth game 7-1, and Pirates pitchers John Candelaria and Kent Tekulve tied the Series in the sixth game by blanking the Orioles 4-0. The all-important seventh game was scheduled to take place in Baltimore on 17 October before a capacity crowd, which included President Jimmy Carter, and an estimated 100 million television viewers.

The Orioles struck first when Rich Dauer hit a home run off Jim Bibby, the Pirates' starter. But Stargell brought the Family back. In his first two at bats Pops had two hits, both to the opposite field because he couldn't pull the hard-throwing Scott McGregor. When he came up in the sixth, another member

ABOVE: *Scott McGregor, the hard-throwing lefty for the Baltimore Orioles.*
TOP: *Baltimore's Ken Singleton is out at home while trying to score from second in the Series.*

of the Family, Bill Robinson, was on first with a single. But McGregor, who had pitched a shutout in the playoffs and had won Game Three for the Orioles, still seemed very much in command, since all through the game his ferocious slider had had the Pirates' batters lunging to no avail at the hard-breaking ball.

For openers McGregor threw Stargell a slider, but this time the ball didn't slide. Stargell jumped all over the pitch and slammed it deep over the rightfield line, giving the Pirates a 2-1 lead and Stargell his third homer of the Series. But the Orioles still had four more at bats.

In the Orioles' sixth and seventh they failed to score, but in the eighth they came up with their best chance to win the Series. Since Game Four, Pirates pitching had held the Orioles hitters to just two runs on 17 hits. Now, with only two more at bats, the Orioles got it going against Grant Jackson. In 1971 Jackson had pitched for the Orioles against the Pirates. Now, pitching for Pittsburgh, he had sailed through the sixth and seventh, but his control faltered in the eighth.

Jackson walks Lee May, a pinch-hitter; then, after Al Brumbry fouls off a number of pitches, Jackson loses him, and Brumbry walks. Chuck Tanner, the Pirates' manager, has little compunction about yanking his pitchers, so on comes Tekulve to try to stop the Orioles and save the Series for the Family.

With two men on, Tekulve gets pinch-hitter Terry Crowley to bounce out to first, with the Orioles' runners advancing to second and third. With Ken Singleton at bat, Tanner orders Tekulve to walk him and load up the bases. That brings up Eddie Murray, one of the most dangerous Orioles hitters, but, to Tanner at least, not as dangerous as Singleton. The walk means that the Pirates can get a force-out at any base. Murray, a switch-hitter, bats left-handed against Tekulve and fouls off the first two Tekulve pitches. He watches as two more go by, just wide. On the fifth pitch, Murray swings, and the ball flies deep to right.

Dave Parker, the big rightfielder for the Pirates adds considerable excitement to the play by completely misjudging the ball. He comes in, sees his error and turns to go back towards the fence. He stumbles and staggers, finally recovers, and then Parker, all 6ft 5in of him, sticks up his mitt, and Eddie Murray's fly ball nestles snugly in, ending the inning and saving the entire Family from a heart attack.

In the Orioles' ninth the Memorial Stadium organ player strikes up, 'It's Now or Never,' hoping to exhort the Birds on to victory. But Kent Tekulve ends any Baltimore dreams as he strikes out Roenicke and Doug DeCinces, and when Pat Kelly lifts an easy fly ball to Omar Moreno in center, it is 'Never' for the Orioles and 'Now' for the Pops and the Family.

Willie Stargell has hit three home runs in this Series, has had seven extra base hits and has provided the Pirates' inspirational leadership. Which goes a long way toward explaining how the Family came from one foot in the grave to winning the 1979 World Series and why Pops is named Most Valuable Player of the year.

OPPOSITE: *The Pirates' ace right-handed relief pitcher, Kent Tekulve.*
BELOW: *The Pittsburgh Pirates celebrate their World Series victory over the Baltimore Orioles as they lead hero Willie Stargell (second from right, top) off the field.*
BOTTOM: *Stargell at bat in the 1979 Series. In Game One his three-run homer broke a 2-2 tie in the eleventh.*

THE ROYALS WIN THE 1980 AMERICAN LEAGUE PENNANT

If a baseball manager were to define the perfect hitter, the definition would probably go like this: He should have an average above .300, have enough power to hit the long ball, getting better than 20 homers a year, and, most important, he should drive in runs – at least 100 a season. And if he can also field, that's a plus.

Surprisingly, in these days of million-dollar salaries, only a few players in baseball could meet those criteria. Some hit the home runs, but their average suffers. Others get the average but don't drive in enough runs or hit home runs in the clutch. Yet in

1980 a young superstar named George Brett had a season that forever established him as one of the truly exceptional hitters in the history of the game. All season long his batting average was close to .400, and all of baseball followed his daily exploits as he tried to become the first hitter since Ted Williams to hit .400 for the year.

All through 1980 George Brett played injured, and there are few finer compliments an athlete can get than to say that 'he played injured.' Hampered by foot injuries and later by a serious hemorrhoid condition, Brett nevertheless led his Kansas City Royals to the

top of the Western Division of the American League. When the Royals went into the playoffs they faced the New York Yankees, who had thrice before beaten the Royals for the American League title.

Brett didn't hit .400 in 1980. He hit .390, driving in 118 runs, but he easily won the league's Most Valuable Player Award, beating out Reggie Jackson of the Yankees and Cecil Cooper of Milwaukee. Jackson had hit 41 home runs,

---

BELOW: *Third baseman George Brett of the Kansas City Royals strikes a long one.*

ABOVE: *George Brett goes after a line drive.*
RIGHT: *Right-handed pitcher Rich Gossage of the New York Yankees was probably the best reliever in the majors in 1980.*

had driven in 111 runs and, for the first time in his career, had reached .300. Cooper led the league in RBI's with 122 and had hit .352, more than good enough to win the batting title in any average year.

The Yankees, now managed by Dick Howser, had won 103 games in the season. In addition to the great year Jackson had had, their pitching, led by Tommy John, with 22 wins, and Ron Guidry, with 17, was solid. And in their bullpen the Yankees had Rich Gossage, the premier relief pitcher in baseball. Gossage, big and powerful through the shoulders, had a fastball that he often threw at more than 100 mph.

Yet despite all this talent, the Yankees were having a desperate time of it in the playoffs, losing the first two games to the Royals. In the final game, the Yankees had battled back to lead 2-1 going into the seventh inning. Tommy John had the Royals hitting into the ground, but in the eighth, he suddenly lost his control. A walk and a single, and the Royals had two on, with two out and George Brett the batter. Manager Dick Howser decided John had had it and brought in Goose Gossage.

This drama brought the huge Yankee Stadium crowd to its feet. The hardest-throwing pitcher in baseball against a power hitter who had just hit .390. The Yankees could walk Brett, but Howser and Gossage didn't even think of it.

Gossage, who sports a big handlebar moustache that makes him seem even more formidable, glares at Brett. Brett stands deep in the batters' box, slightly crouched, bat cocked, eyes on Gossage. The big righthander straightens up, ignores the base runners and throws. Brett swings at the hard fastball, and the crack of his bat tells all that it is gone. Deep into the New York night the gleaming ball flies towards the rightfield stands, to land in the third deck of the huge stadium. As Brett rounds the bases, Yankees fans, never noted for their generosity, stand and applaud in tribute to a great moment. The greatest hitter in the game has beaten the greatest relief pitcher, and

the Royals have won their first American League championship.

For Dick Howser, whose Yankees had won more games than any Yankees teams since 1961, the loss was a bitter disappointment. His understanding owner, George Steinbrenner, fired him and replaced him with Billy Martin. But for George Brett that classic confrontation with Gossage was the capstone of a season that would probably guarantee his admission to the Hall of Fame.

If baseball history were written like the script of a well-made play the Royals would doubtless have gone on to beat the Phillies in the World Series, but Brett's illnesses slowed him down, whereas the Phillies' National League MVP Mike Schmidt, the great Pete Rose, Cy Young Award-winner Steve Carlton and the fine reliever Tug McGraw were all in top form. And in its own way, the Phillies' triumph was dramatic enough, for it was the team's very first World Championship. It had taken them just 105 years to get it.

LEFT: *Tommy John, the phenomenal left-hander for the New York Yankees.*
OPPOSITE: *Batting star Mike Schmidt of the Philadelphia Phillies.*
BELOW: *George Brett is embraced by teammates after his three-run homer.*

The Great Pine Tar Rhubarb

There is a rule in baseball that a bat cannot have any foreign substance on or in it. The rule was designed to prevent hitters from hollowing out the inside of the bat head and putting in cork or some other substance that would make the ball travel farther when hit. As interpreted, the rule applies particularly to any areas of the bat 18 or more inches from the handle. When the Kansas City Royals traveled to Yankee Stadium for a series in July 1983 little did they know that they would soon be participants in an absurd little drama involving the same rule. The stars of the show would be a hitter, George Brett; a manager, Billy Martin; an umpire; and 20 inches of pine tar.

George Brett has hit some of his most memorable home runs against the New York Yankees in Yankee Stadium. His three-run homer off Goose Gossage in the 1980 playoffs was only the most famous. In another playoff game he hit three homers. But never had George Brett hit a home run that set off such an explosion as the one he hit on 24 July 1983.

Going into the ninth inning, the Royals trailed the Yankees 4-3. With one man on, Brett slammed a two-run homer – or so he thought. As he watched the ball sail deep into the rightfield stands, Brett dropped his bat at home and began his home run trot around the bases. Greeted at home by his jubilant teammates, Brett jogged over to the bench, sat down and looked out on the field. What he saw was a spirited discussion at home plate.

Shrewd, feisty Billy Martin, now back for his third stint as Yankees manager under the benign (?) despotism of King George III, had run out to the plate and was furiously expostulating with the umpire. Apparently he was raising a question about Brett's homer, but what it could be, no one could imagine. Still less could they have imagined that it had to do with the pine tar on Brett's bat. Everyone knew that Brett liked to put pine tar on the handle of his bat to reduce slippage. So did lots of other batters.

OPPOSITE: *George Brett of the Kansas City Royals at bat.*
BELOW: *Yankee manager Billy Martin holds a conference with an umpire.*

After a time the umpire walked over to the Royals' dugout and asked to see George Brett's bat. When it was given to him, he looked at it and then walked back to home plate with Martin and Dick Howser, the Royals manager, at his heels. Using the bat, the umpire measured from the back of home plate to the front of home plate, a distance of 18 inches. The pine tar on George Brett's bat extended more than 18 inches from the handle. With prompting from Billy Martin, the umpire now told Howser that Brett had used an illegal substance on his bat and that therefore the homer didn't count, that Brett was out and that the Yankees had won the game 4-3.

Brett explodes from the dugout, racing towards the umpire. Teammates try to stop him, but Brett's rage gets him close enough so that his words are fully understood. The Royals literally drag Brett away into the locker room. In the Yankees' locker room, Billy Martin explains to the press what happened.

He tells them everything about the little-known substance rule and, with all the earnestness of a truth-seeker, says, 'I was only helping the umpire understand and enforce the rule.' When members of the press ask how long he knew Brett's bat had pine tar longer than 18 inches, Martin's re-action is simply to smile. The Yankees had played the Royals a few days earlier and Brett was playing with the same bat.

Sanity and justice were preserved when, four days later, Lee MacPhail, president of the American League, overruled the umpire and gave the home run to Brett, ordering the game to be completed from the point of the dispute. In other words, the Yankees had three outs to try to win.

George Steinbrenner's reaction was swift and predictable. 'It sure tests our faith in our leadership,' George III stormed. 'If the Yankees lose the division by one game, I wouldn't want to be Lee MacPhail living in New York.

ABOVE: *Slugger George Brett of the Royals with his pine-tarred bat.*

Maybe he should go house-hunting in Kansas City.'

On 18 August, an open date for both clubs, they completed the game begun on 24 July. It took 12 minutes, and the Royals won 5-4. Bowie Kuhn conducted a hearing because of Stein-brenner's remarks about MacPhail and ended by fining Steinbrenner $250,000 and ordering the Yankees to pay an extra $50,000 for legal fees.

All in all, in 1983 George Stein-brenner was fined a total of $355,000. He had picked up $5000 for being involved in a name-calling contest with the Chicago White Sox owner, Eddie Einhorn, and $50,000 for questioning the integritity of National League umpires. With Kuhn's decision George set an authentic single-season baseball record, and one that may never be broken – except by Steinbrenner.

STEVE CARLTON WINS HIS 300TH GAME

Over the years there have been many players – usually pitchers – given the sobriquet 'Lefty.' Two names that instantly come to mind are Lefty Grove and Lefty Gomez, both Hall of Fame pitchers. Five years after his eligibility, Steve Carlton will doubtless join them in Cooperstown. He won't be inducted because he was a favorite of the media, but because he was the dominant left-handed pitcher in baseball for almost two decades. The nickname 'Lefty' was seldom used by the media when talking about Steve Carlton, but whenever one of his teammates or opponents mentioned 'Lefty' there was seldom much doubt about whom they were talking.

On a Friday night in August 1983, at Busch Memorial Stadium in St Louis, Steve Carlton joined 16 other pitchers by winning his 300th game. And by winning the 300th against the Cardinals, Carlton rubbed salt into an old wound. For Carlton had pitched for the St Louis Cardinals when he first came

BELOW: *Pitcher Steve 'Lefty' Carlton of the Philadelphia Phillies.*

into baseball. He was the ace of their staff after Bob Gibson, but in the early 70s, Gussie Busch, the patriarch of the

OPPOSITE: *Carlton pitching against the Cardinals in his 300th victory.*
BELOW: *Pitcher Tom Seaver when he was with the Chicago White Sox – another 300 game winner.*
BOTTOM: *Fireball-pitching Nolan Ryan.*

Cardinals, would not give his young star the kind of praise Carlton felt – correctly – he had earned. When Carlton took his beef to the press, the owner of Anhauser-Busch and the Cardinals sold Steve Carlton to the Philadelphia Phillies.

To call the selling of Carlton one of the less inspired deals in baseball history is like describing World War II as a

disagreement. Without him the Cardinals would go almost 10 years before winning a World Series. Carlton has been named the winner of the Cy Young Award three times since leaving the Cardinals, and in 1980, his pitching brought the Phillies their first and only World Championship. Along with Nolan Ryan and Tom Seaver, Carlton became one of the leading strikeouts artists in baseball history.

In the 1983 season Carlton had struggled a bit – for him. Coming into the game in St Louis he had a record of 14-15, but his strikeouts were among the league leaders. In the first three innings Carlton shut out the Cardinals and gave the Phillies the lead by driving in a run in the second. But in the fourth he made a mistake of a kind seldom seen in his career: He gave up a home run to David Green on a slider that didn't slide. But the Phillies, on a hot streak of seven straight wins, got three more runs, and Carlton settled down to keep the Cardinals scoreless going into the last of the eighth.

Now Carlton showed the St Louis crowd what they had missed during the last decade. He gave up a triple to Ozzie Smith and then struck out the next two batters and got the last one to bounce back to the mound. It was Carlton's last inning. He had struck out 12 Cardinals; now he sat in the dugout as teammate Al Holland kept the Cardinals from scoring in the ninth.

Carlton exchanged handshakes with the rest of the Phillies, walked over to a special box where his wife was seated and hugged her. Surprisingly, there was little fanfare in Busch Stadium. Maybe under orders from on high, the Cardinals' public address announcer did not tell the St Louis fans that Steve Carlton had just won his 300th game.

The Phillies went on to win their second National League flag in the '80s, but the Baltimore Orioles easily defeated them in the World Series, four games to one. Carlton's great career wound down, and in 1986, after he couldn't seem to get anyone out, the great pitcher was given his outright release from the Phillies. He hooked up with the San Francisco Giants but was ineffective. The Giants were in a pennant race and needed Carlton's spot on the roster to bring in a younger pitcher. On 8 August, pitching for the Giants, Steve Carlton struck out his 4000th hitter. He lost the game and afterwards called a press conference to announce his retirement.

Only Nolan Ryan had struck out more hitters, but Carlton's 4000 strikeouts in a career put him ahead of all others. No need now to ask whom people mean when they are talking about 'Lefty.'

PETE ROSE TOPS TY COBB'S RECORD

Pete Rose's life is baseball. Once when asked by columnist Red Smith the year of his birth, Pete replied, 'It was 1941, the year DiMaggio got 56 consecutive hits.' When Rose asked Smith when he began writing for a newspaper, Red said it was 1927. Commented Rose, putting the Pulitzer Prize writer's debut into perspective, 'The year Ruth hit his 60 home runs.'

Of all the players who have played the game, Peter Edward Rose is perhaps the closest in temperament and talent to the great Ty Cobb. Like the Georgia Peach, Rose hates to lose and will do anything to win. Like Cobb, Rose is mainly a singles or doubles hitter who can also hit for power when he wants to.

As the 1985 season began, all of sports watched as Rose chased after a record that many thought as sacrosanct as Ruth's 60 season home runs and his 714 lifetime homers, Walter Johnson's 3508 strikeouts or Cy Young's 511 lifetime wins. In fact, most of the records set by the famous oldtimers had already been passed by 1985, the great exceptions being Cobb's lifetime hit record and Cy Young's lifetime wins.

Young's record looked as inaccessible as ever in 1985, but now, incredibly, Cobb's 4191 hits had begun to look as if it might be within Pete Rose's reach.

Back in the late 1970s, when he was playing for the Philadelphia Phillies, Rose maintained that if he could average 150 hits a season, he had a shot. In early April 1984, Pete Rose, now with the Montréal Exposes, smacked a double off Jerry Koosman of the Phillies for his 4000th base hit. Only Ty Cobb was in that class. Now Pete had to get 192 more to best the record no one thought would ever be broken.

In August 1984 Pete Rose returned to his home town as player-manager of the Cincinnati Reds. When the '84 season ended Pete Rose had broken Carl Yastrzemski's record for lifetime

BELOW: *Pete Rose of the Cincinnati Reds – always the hustler.*

But the real story of 1985 was Pete Rose's assault on Cobb's 4191. And as media coverage of Rose's progress intensified, a new generation of baseball fans became re-acquainted with the legendary figure whose record Rose was pursuing. It wasn't just the amazing statistics – the .367 batting average for 27 years of play, the 892 stolen bases and all the rest – that made Cobb so fascinating. It was the man himself – the finest, fiercest player in the history of the game. Eddie Collings, the Hall of Fame second baseman whose own career spanned most of Cobb's, once said that Cobb 'could have chased half the present-day players out of the league with his spikes.' (In fact, when the Hall of Fame was opened in 1939, the first memento displayed was a pair of Cobb's infamous spikes.)

Once, while attending a ballgame in Mantle & Maris era, Cobb was asked by a sportswriter what he thought he'd hit in a modern game.

'Oh, I'd probably hit .340 or so,' said Cobb.

'So you think today's pitchers would hold you below your average?' asked the writer.

'Well,' said the Georgia Peach, 'you have to remember I'm almost 70 now.'

Inevitably there were a good many people who didn't want to see the great Cobb's lifetime hitting record broken.

ABOVE: *Rod Carew of the California Angels – another pure hitter.*
RIGHT: *Pete Rose studying the pitcher as he waits for his turn at bat.*

games played, broken Ty Cobb's record for singles and broken Stan Musial's record for doubles. Now only Cobb's lifetime hits escaped his grasp.

If doing something that puts you in the record book almost invariably constitutes a great moment in sport, then 1985 was a year of great moments in baseball. Early in August Tom Seaver, now no longer a Met but pitching for the Chicago White Sox, won his 300th game when he beat the Yankees 4-1 in New York. In the last game of the season the Yankees' Phil Niekro accomplished the same thing when he shut out Toronto 8-0. In so doing both men crossed that invisible barrier that separates the great pitchers from the super-great and took their places in a stratosphere to which only 16 other men had ever before ascended.

On the same afternoon that Seaver won his 300th game, on the other side of the country, the Angels' Rod Carew performed the batter's equivalent of Tom Terrific's accomplishment by getting his 3000th base hit. In his illustrious career Carew has won seven batting titles. Only Honus Wagner and Ty Cobb won more, and only Stan Musial won as many.

And perhaps no one was more sympathetic to this nostalgic sentiment than Pete Rose himself, for Rose yielded to none in his admiration of Cobb. But Rose also knew that nothing could be more fatal to baseball than attempting to make it stand still. If he thought he could top Cobb's 4191, he owed it to himself, to the sport and to Ty Cobb to try.

On the afternoon of 8 September Pete Rose and the Cincinnati Reds played the Chicago Cubs in the friendly confines of Wrigley Field. Rose was two hits away from tying Cobb's

Rose breaks Ty Cobb's record 4191 hits – 11 September 1985. Ranking third was Hank Aaron, whose total was 3771.

record. Facing a rookie pitcher, Rose singled in his first at bat. Now he was one away. With a huge crowd urging him on, Rose came to bat in the fifth against Reggie Patterson and singled hard to right: the record was tied. He struck out in the eighth, and then the rains came. For two hours they soaked Wrigley Field, until finally the umpires called the game with the score tied.

The Reds returned to Cincinnati and opened a series against the San Diego Padres. Rose didn't play in the opener, and on the night of 10 September he went hitless. On the next night Riverfront Stadium was packed, with every seat sold and standing-room only filled. The Cincinnati Fire Department was forced to close the gates as a matter of safety.

The huge crowd cheered Rose as he came to bat in the last of the first. He was playing in his 23rd season, and this at bat was his 13,768th. Batting left-handed and facing rightie Eric Snow of the Padres, Pete Rose lined a hard single to left field. And the record was finally his – 4192!

Pete Rose stands on first base as the thunderous applause swirls around him. He tips his hat and accepts the congratulations of his teammates, and when the Padres' leftfielder throws the ball in, the umpire gives it to Pete. Everyone expects Pete to go into the dugout. But he rolls the ball over to the Reds' dugout and takes his lead at first. After all, there is still a ball game to be won. Ty Cobb would have understood perfectly.

THE 1986 WORLD SERIES

When the 1986 major league baseball season began, the New York Mets manager, Davy Johnson, said he expected his team to win the National League pennant. They did, running away with the Eastern Division by a lopsided 20 games and squeaking by the Houston Astros in six games to win the National League title.

In the American League the Boston Red Sox were not expected to win anything. But as the season progressed, the Sox surprised everyone by getting off to a fast start and keeping it through the season. In the American League Playoffs they fought and won a cliffhanger duel with the California Angels and so went on to face the mighty Mets – favored 11-5 to win – in the Series.

The Series opened in Shea Stadium in New York, and the Red Sox proceeded to win the first two games! But when the Series went to Boston's Fenway Park, the odds-makers still thought the Mets would win. And, in fact, the Mets came back and won two

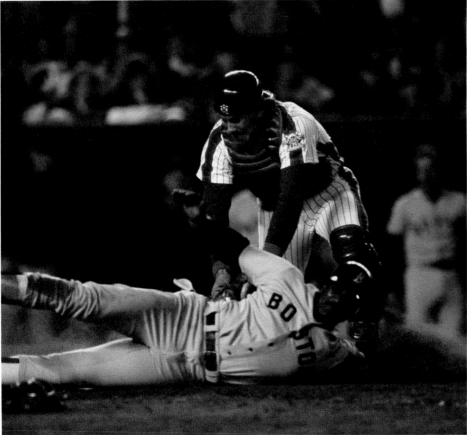

ABOVE: *In Game Six of the 1986 World Series Ray Knight drove in the first run of the Mets' winning rally.*
LEFT: *Catcher Gary Carter of the Mets puts out Red Sox outfielder Jim Rice in a close call at home plate.*

of the three in Boston, forcing the Series back to Shea Stadium. But, still, all the Sox needed was one win, and the Series was theirs.

In Game Six the 1986 World Series became the stuff of legend. The Red Sox needed only one game to win their first World Series since 1918, when the star had been their pitcher, George Herman (Babe) Ruth. Three times after Ruth was sold to the Yankees the Red Sox had played in the World Series. Each time the Series went seven games, and each time, heartbreakingly, the Red Sox had come up on the short end of the stick. For Red Sox fans, this litany of failure was as easy to repeat as saying grace before meals. But now they had a real chance.

Pitching in Game Six for the Red Sox was Roger Clemens, their sure Cy

Young Award winner (and eventual MVP). For the Mets, it was Bob Ojeda, a former Red Sox, dealt to the Mets in the off-season. The Red Sox staked Clemens to a three-run lead, and Clemens was throwing aspirins at the Mets. But he was also wild and by the seventh inning had developed a painful blister on his hand. So manager John McNamara went to his bullpen and brought in Kevin Schiraldi, the ace of the Red Sox relief staff.

With a man on first, Schiraldi threw away a bunt, and the Mets had men on first and second. The Mets then got a man to third, and Gary Carter hit a sacrifice fly on a 3-0 count to tie the score at three all. In the tenth inning, the Red Sox regained the lead when Dave Henderson nailed a 0-1 pitch from Mets reliever Rick Agulera. Then they added another run, to end the top of the tenth leading 5-3. They needed just three more outs.

Schiraldi quickly got two outs, and now the Bosox were one out away from ending their ancient travail. The Red Sox bench was standing, smiling, ready to celebrate. The Mets were quiet and tense.

Gary Carter, the Mets catcher, comes up and, on a 2-1 count, singles to left.

Then Kevin Mitchell, batting for the pitcher, comes to the plate. Mitchell loops a single to center, and the Mets have two on. Schiraldi gets two strikes on Ray Knight, the Mets third baseman. Only one strike away. But Knight lines a fastball to center, and Carter comes in to score. Now it is 5-4, Red Sox. At this point McNamara replaces Schiraldi with Bob Stanley. Can Stanley pitch the winning out? Will this be a pitcher's dream, or a pitcher's nightmare?

The batter is Mookie Wilson, a bad-ball hitter. Stanley throws a ball and follows it with a strike. Another ball and another strike. The Mets have runners on first and third. Stanley throws a breaking ball and Wilson fouls it off. Another curve and again a foul. Still one strike away from victory. Now Stanley tries a running fastball that should break away from the hitter. But it doesn't break. It runs in on Wilson, who bails out of the batters' box and momentarily blocks the view of catcher Rich Gedman. The ball is past Gedman and rolling to the screen, and the Mets' Mitchell scores, as Ray Knight races to second. Now the score is tied, and the Mets fans are going crazy.

The count is three and two on Wilson. He looks down the first base line and sees that first baseman Bill Buckner is playing far in back of the bag. Wilson knows that injuries to Buckner's ankles have impaired his ability to run. Stanley pitches and Wilson swings. He tops the ball, and it slowly bounces down the first base line, fair. Knight is running from second to third, and Buckner is limping in towards the ball as it bounces towards him. The ball bounces over the base, but Buckner still isn't quite in position to catch it, and it trickles under his outstretched mitt. Knight continues past third, as the ball slowly

RIGHT: *Californian Bob Ojeda joined the Sox in 1980 and established an ERA of 4.27 in his first five years with Boston. But it was as a Met that he pitched in the crucial sixth game of the 1986 World Series.*

BELOW: *Red Sox catcher Rich Gedman vainly waits for the throw as the Mets' Gary Carter slides safely home. Carter started with Montréal in 1974 and joined the Mets in 1984. Gedman has played for Boston since 1980.*

rolls into short right field. Knight scores and the Mets win! To make the whole thing more painful for the Sox, the scoreboard inadvertently flashes the message 'Congratulations Boston Red Sox.'

The seventh game was put off until Monday. At first the Mets again trailed 3-0, but in the sixth inning they tied it. You could almost feel the Red Sox's hopes beginning to crumble. Poor Kevin Schiraldi came in to face that tie score in the seventh. Ray Knight was up, and he hammered a fastball deep into the leftfield bullpen. Mets, 4-3. Then they scored twice more. The Red Sox got close, scoring twice in the eighth, but the Mets put them away in the ninth, and that was that. The Mets had won the 1986 Series.

The Red Sox could take pride in the way they had won the American League flag. But they would probably never be able to forget that awful sixth game when the ghosts of Red Sox defeats past rose up and delivered to the New Englanders yet another reminder of how very hard life can be.

INDEX

JOHN WAYNE

JOHN WAYNE

The Legend and the Man

An Exclusive Look Inside Duke's Archive

Essay by **Patricia Bosworth**

Foreword by **Martin Scorsese**

Remembrance by **Maureen O'Hara**

Interview with **Ron Howard**

Remembrance by **Ronald Reagan**

pH **powerHouse Books**

Brooklyn, NY

Photo credits

Nancy Hogue: 11, 113 (bottom), 114 (top), 115, 119, 120, 123 (bottom), 124 (bottom), 128 (top), 129, 133, 137.
International New Service: 59.
Ronald C Modra: 7, 117, 121, 125, 126, 127, 130, 134 (top), 136, 139 (both), 140, 141, 142.
National Baseball Library: 8, 9 (top), 10 (top), 12 (top left), 13 (top), 15, 16, 17 (center and bottom), 19, 20 (bottom), 21 (top), 22, 23, 24, 25 (bottom), 26 (top right and bottom left), 27 (top), 28 (bottom), 29 (bottom), 30 (top), 32, 35 (top), 36 (top left), 39 (bottom), 45 (top), 46 (bottom right), 50 (bottom), 52 (top), 54, 63 (top), 64 (bottom), 72, 75 (top), 80 (right), 82, 83 (top), 87 (top), 97 (top), 99 (right), 101 (left), 105 (top), 107 (bottom), 108 (top), 111 (bottom), 122, 132.
UPI/Bettmann Newsphotos: 1, 3, 6, 9 (bottom), 10 (bottom), 12 (top right and bottom), 12 (top right and bottom), 13 (bottom), 14, 17 (top), 18, 20 (top), 21 (bottom), 25 (top), 26 (bottom right), 27 (bottom), 28 (top), 29 (top), 30 (bottom), 31, 33, 34, 35 (bottom), 36 (top right and bottom), 37, 38, 39 (top), 40, 41, 42, 43, 44, 45 (bottom left and top right), 46 (top and bottom left), 47, 48, 49, 50 (top), 51, 52 (bottom), 53, 55, 56, 57, 58, 60, 61, 62, 63 (bottom), 64 (top), 65, 66, 67, 68, 69, 70, 71, 73, 74, 75 (bottom), 76, 77, 78, 79, 80 (left), 81, 83 (bottom), 84, 85, 86, 87 (bottom), 88, 89, 90, 91, 92, 93, 94, 95, 96, 97 (bottom), 98, 99 (left), 100, 101 (right), 102, 103, 104, 105 (bottom), 96, 97 (bottom), 98, 99 (left), 100, 101 (right), 102, 103, 104, 105 (bottom), 106, 107 (top), 108 (bottom), 109, 110, 111 (top), 112, 113 (top), 114 (bottom), 116, 118, 123 (top), 124 (top), 128 (bottom), 131, 134 (bottom), 135, 138.

Acknowledgements

The publisher would like to thank the following people who have helped in the preparation of this book: Design 23 who designed it; John Kirk who edited it; Donna Cornell Muntz, who did the picture research; Cynthia Klein, who prepared the index. Special thanks go to Pat Kelly Photo Collection Manager, and staff at The National Baseball Hall of Fame and Museum, Inc; and to Katherine Graubard and staff at UPI/ Bettmann.